Garden
Artistry

Garden Artistry

*Secrets of Planting and
Designing a Small Garden*

HELEN DILLON

A HORTICULTURE BOOK

MACMILLAN • USA

PAGE 1

Allium aflatunense (bottom left), geraniums, and erodiums beside the path leading to the Iris Garden. Red Salvia microphylla var. neurepia is tucked into a sheltered corner to the left of the wrought iron arch.

TITLE PAGE

Hellebores are greedy plants. Two buckets of mixed fresh topsoil, well-rotted manure, garden compost, and leaf mold (in any proportion) plus bonemeal are worked into the planting hole for each plant.

OPPOSITE

Bergenia 'Ballawley' can be used as a garden thermometer—the leaves blush red with cold and turn green overnight when the weather warms up.

MACMILLAN
A Simon & Schuster Macmillan Company
1633 Broadway
New York, NY 10019-6785

Copyright © 1995 by Helen Dillon

Photography © 1995 by Helen Dillon and Diane Tomlinson (others where noted)

MACMILLAN is a registered trademark of Macmillan, Inc.

A *Horticulture* Book

An affiliate of *Horticulture*, the Magazine of American Gardening

Library of Congress Cataloging-in-Publication Data
Dillon, Helen.
  Garden artistry: secrets of designing and planting
  a small garden/Helen Dillon; photography by
  Helen Dillon & Diane Tomlinson.
      p.   cm.
  Includes bibliographical references (p. 186) and index.
  ISBN 0-02-860379-6 (hc)
  1. Landscape gardening. 2. Gardens—Design.
  3. Plants, Ornamental. 4. Landscape gardening—
  Ireland. 5. Gardens—Ireland—Design. 6. Plants,
  Ornamental—Ireland.   I. Title.
  SB473.D54   1995
  635.9—dc20   95-12909
                                               CIP

Manufactured in the United States of America

10 9 8 7 6 5 4 3 2 1

Photography Credits

PHOTOGRAPHS BY DIANE TOMLINSON APPEAR ON PAGES 1, 2, 6 (CENTER), 7 (ALL), 8, 10, 15, 16, 18, 19, 20, 22, 26, 28, 31, 32, 35, 38–39, 42–43, 44, 46, 48, 54, 56, 63, 64, 71, 76, 78–79, 81, 85, 86, 88–89, 90, 98, 99, 100–101, 103, 104, 110, 112–113, 115, 116, 117, 118–119, 121, 122, 123, 124, 125, 132–133, 141, 142, 144–145, 146, 148–149, 151, 154, 155, 159, 160, 161, 162, 163, 164, 171, 176, 184–185.

PHOTOGRAPHS BY HELEN DILLON APPEAR ON PAGES 6 (LEFT AND RIGHT), 50–51, 69, 72–73, 91, 108–109, 128, 129, 130, 134–135, 137, 138, 156–157, 168–169, 173.

PHOTOGRAPHS BY CHARLES NELSON APPEAR ON PAGES 36, 66, 94, 120, 166–167.

PHOTOGRAPHS BY CYNTHIA WOODYARD APPEAR ON PAGES 57, 60–61, 178.

PHOTOGRAPHS BY JONATHAN SEARLE ON PAGES 5, 174.

PHOTOGRAPH BY GEORGE LÉVÊQUE APPEARS ON PAGE 59.

PAGES 6–7

(LEFT TO RIGHT):

The Alpine House in January, with Narcissus romieuxii 'Julia Jane.' (See page 137 for full caption.)

The left-handed border in summer, concealing countless bulbs now dormant. (See page 9 for full caption.)

Johnny-jump-up (Viola tricolor). (See page 136 for full caption.)

Cyclamen coum *with Crocus tommasinianus. (See page 131 for full caption.)*

Auriculas. (See page 98 for full caption.)

The raised bed in the Sundial Garden. (See page 21 for full caption.)

Contents

Introduction

༄༅

In this book I describe my attempt at the impossible — to reconcile the collector's instinct with the desire to make a garden that is pleasant to be in, even if you don't know the name of a single plant. This is a challenging task because a collector's garden is all too frequently a cabinet of curiosities, a glorious confection of plants, some planted in splendid isolation as befits their rarity, most dotted about anywhere there is a gap. Squads of smart labels in regimented rows embellish the flower beds. As you can imagine, this approach does not lead to an atmosphere of serenity.

All gardeners are collectors to a certain extent. For some, it may be all things variegated: The sight of a leaf striped in white, splashed in cream, or ever so slightly mottled in yellow brings immoderate excitement. Others are lured by alpine plants, and the more challenging they are to grow, the better. Collectors may have the urge to own every known species and cultivar in a single genus, and then to discuss the minute differences thereof with like-minded addicts. Or perhaps they simply fall in love with Shirley poppies and from then on want each and every poppy, from Himalayan blue poppies (*Meconopsis* species) and flamboyant Orientals (*Papaver orientale*) right down to the Welsh poppy (*Meconopsis cambrica*) — charm itself, but a true weed at heart.

The left-handed border in summer, concealing countless bulbs now dormant. Invariably, many bulbs are dug up during the autumn upheavals, but I just push them back and hope for the best.

OVERLEAF

By November, the sun is so low and the weather so cool that plants have stopped growing, but I'm still busy dividing plants and sorting out the borders.

For the irrepressible collector the thrill is threefold. You learn about a plant — by reading about it, seeing it in somebody else's garden, or listening to the gardening cognoscenti discussing it. Then ensues the chase, with attendant excitement. And finally the moment of acquisition. Bliss.

The collector's garden may thus contain an astonishing assortment of bulbs, herbaceous perennials, trees, shrubs, annuals, biennials, and roses (old-fashioned or otherwise). To organize this array of plants — remembering the soil and light requirements, aspect, season of bloom, height, spread, and color of each — is more difficult than a jigsaw puzzle, because no sooner do you finish a section than the pieces move off of their own accord. And the best-laid plans are often confounded by plants imbued with such uncontrollable wanderlust that they have no intention of staying where you put them in the first place.

Some sort of order needs to be imposed on this vast accumulation. The principal ways of doing this are, first, to give the garden a fairly formal design that will contain exuberant plantings within a strong framework; second, to group plants according to their cultural need, creating special areas for those with particular requirements, such as alpines, lime haters, shade lovers, or plants needing a sheltered spot; and third, to group plants by color.

I feel emphatically that a formal design, on however modest a scale, allows the collecting spirit free rein. You can get away with placing umpteen plants higgledy-piggledy provided they are contained within strict, architectural lines.

Even if a plant is the only known example in Ireland, if all it does is lead a miserable existence in a muddy yogurt container (along with several hundred similar victims nearby), I'd rather not have it. I not only want the plant to flower and fruit and glow with health as it would in the wild, I want to make it look comfortable in a garden setting.

To combat the threat of garden chaos, a collector not only needs to be passionate about something, but also professional and methodical. My garden in Dublin was started in 1972. I was then at the delirious beginner's stage — whenever I saw a plant, my motto was "Buy it and see." After four years, I became a bit more organized, and since 1976, records have been kept of every plant added to the garden, with a note indicating whence it came. It makes soul-searching reading: the plants that die; those given up because they were not worth growing; the one-and-the-same plant acquired under no less than four different names; the twenty-three different alliums of which few survived onion neck rot; and the ravishing plants I have fallen for over and over again, such as *Paraquilegia anemonoïdes* (Zone 5) — plants I'm determined, just once, to grow well. The records are in a box I hesitate to open, so full is it of memories of gardeners and their gardens.

Visitors assume that one night, in a flash of creativity, I designed this garden. Not so. My method is to wait until some part of it annoys me and then take action. I'm usually satisfied with it in winter and spring, but by late summer all the mistakes show. Endless adjustments have taken place; in the paths, the shapes of beds, and, above all, in the planting.

The Garden at 45 Sandford Road

The story of how a garden began is often a tiresome tale of rampant nettles, brambles, and weeds, followed by heroic descriptions of how the owner hacked his way through dim-lit undergrowth. It concludes with a glowing description of what the new garden looks like — all created despite aphids, appalling soil, frost pockets, bad drainage, wind tunnels, marauding cats, and previously unrecorded fungi. My story, on similar lines, goes as follows.

We inherited roses, apple trees, a wobbly forties-style greenhouse, various henhouses, a large bed of bearded irises, a vegetable patch, and a so-called rockery, in reality a pile of stones in the middle of the lawn. With the heady excitement of actually owning a garden at last, I was far too cautious to change anything. I loved every little bit of it, weeds and all. In deepest ignorance, yet with the help of Sean, a taxi driver who was a gardener manqué at heart, I did little at first except remove the rockery and henhouses, cut the grass, and tidy up. Meanwhile, with reckless enthusiasm, I bought every plant in sight, with no thought whatsoever as to its suitability to my soil or climate.

The garden, surrounded by stone walls and situated thirty minutes' walk from the center of Dublin, covers less than an acre. The soil is slightly alkaline, light and easy to work, but it has been under cultivation for so long (the house was built in 1830) that it needs continual additions of humus. Annual rainfall is less than thirty inches. The climate corresponds to USDA Zone 8 and is comparable to that of Seattle, but our summers are not as hot and the air is always humid. Occasionally we have a stinker of a winter, and the temperature drops as low as 10 degrees Fahrenheit. The latitude of

Hedera helix 'Buttercup' cloaks one of a pair of sphinxes flanking the steps to the lawn. Surreptitious snipping keeps the ivy under control.

OVERLEAF
Bulbs in the spring flower border, looking south from the house. Beginning with snow-drops and crocuses in February, there is an ever-changing carpet of pushkinias, chiono-doxas, scillas, muscari, dog's-tooth violets, fritillarias, daffodils, tulips, and alliums that continues until late May.

The pale pink storksbill Erodium pelargoni-iflorum, *at the edge of the path leading to the Iris Garden, seeds itself in just the right places and flowers nonstop from March to November.*

Dublin is the same as that of Newfoundland and Hudson Bay, so even at its zenith the sun is low in the sky, although in the long summer evenings you can garden until almost midnight.

The main garden is at the back of the house and faces south. Granite steps, guarded by a pair of sphinxes, lead up from a wide sunny terrace to a central lawn that is flanked by two borders. On the far sides, meandering paths separate these borders from two further borders that follow the boundary walls along the garden's periphery.

Thus there are four large beds, extending at right angles to the house, planted according to color. On the extreme right, looking from the house, is a bed composed of silver foliage and flowers in pastel shades, including quite a lot of pale pink. Next is the Blue Border. On the opposite side of the lawn is the Red Border, and on the extreme left is a border mainly for spring flowers. In the middle of this last bed is an area planted with silver foliage mingled with magenta flowers, including some best described as "difficult pink." My arrangement of color may appear the result of careful planning, but the reality is somewhat different; many is the time some poor plant has been hauled out of the ground in full flower and hastily transplanted elsewhere.

The perspective of the long, rectangular lawn is false: In an effort to make the garden appear larger than it is, the area of grass narrows slightly toward the far end. This works rather well. But as much as I love strong, formal lines in a garden, the moment they are in place, I want plants to spill over the edges and soften them. As you can imagine, the tumbling plants caused patches of bare earth until we put in a sandstone mowing edge at either side. The lawn is fussed over by my husband, Val, who feeds it every three weeks in summer. Arguments are ongoing as to whether the lawn or the flowers should be watered; as soon as I look the other way, the hose is moved to the grass.

Pansies, artimesia, and hebe growing in a paved area in the Iris Garden.

At the distant end of the lawn is a circular pool set in a semicircle of wrought iron arches. Beyond is an arcade cloaked by roses and clematis, extending the long axis of the lawn and framing the view of a statue of Diana.

Tucked behind the main garden are three small gardens, invisible from the house, known respectively as the Iris Garden (though there isn't a single iris in it), the Sundial Garden, and the Oval lawn.

The Iris Garden came about because I couldn't stand the way weeds infiltrated around the rhizomes of the tall bearded irises. So I made a paved area, leaving spaces between the stones for each cultivar. The irises were duly corralled. Although this made weeding easier (I didn't have to clamber into the middle of the iris bed), the irises didn't stay for long: their flowering season was too short, so all except my favorite — an anonymous light blue — were given away. I began to collect the dwarf bearded kinds instead.

From this paved area you walk under an arch of wrought iron trellis to the Sundial Garden, a large raised bed encircling a graveled area, with a sundial in

the middle. When you mention raised beds, people become very shifty unless they happen to be alpine enthusiasts. But, rock plants aside, this part of the garden contains many choice little herbaceous plants, far too refined to be risked among the hoi polloi of the border proper. In a raised bed they are at least safe from the galumphing foot.

The Oval Lawn, separated from the Sundial Garden by the tunnel of clematis and roses, is in the far left-hand corner of the garden. This area never quite seemed to work. Whatever I did was no improvement. The position of the path was always being changed; more and more plants were added. Everybody was consulted about what should be done. Perhaps another small tree, yet another evergreen, or some plants with bold foliage would do the trick? Large pots of plants were trundled round to different positions. Finally I realized that the problem was simply due to the vast miscellany of plants. Whenever I couldn't decide where to plant something, this was where it ended up. A plain green carpet of grass was the only thing to counterbalance the different flower colors and leaf shapes.

So, much as the collector grudged parting with so much growing space, the lawn was laid. The oval of grass is peaceful. I like this bit of the garden, but I'm still fiddling with the plants. At the moment the surrounding beds are mostly planted with yellow, orange, and blue flowers. In the corner, shaded by the north-facing wall, is a series of raised beds, some filled with lime-free soil, and all colonized by the Scottish flame flower (*Tropaeolum speciosum;* Zone 7). Here grow trilliums, hardy orchids, toad lilies, and choice members of the Ericaceae, such as *Menziesia cilliicalyx* (Zone 6) and *Phyllodoce aleutica* (Zone 2).

OVERLEAF
This area, partly shaded by the elderly 'Bramley' apple, used to contain a miscellaneous jumble of plants. It only became more tranquil when we laid a plain oval of grass in the center.

To the right of the garden, near the house, are a Victorian-style greenhouse, built in 1976, a small alpine house, more raised beds, and a little terrace, paved with Victorian tiles (the site of an earlier greenhouse), protected by a trellised wall. A little conceit, in the form of a gothic-style window, permits a view through to the border beyond.

The greenhouse contains an ever-changing congregation of plants. Here they almost need an Award of Merit to qualify for a permanent home. Many is the plant that's been given its marching orders for growing too big. *Jasminum polyanthum*, however, the oldest resident, has a place of honor. On warm spring days its heavenly scent fills the greenhouse, overflowing through cracks in the windows and seeping out under the door to the nearby potting shed. The temperature of the greenhouse is kept just above freezing, with a bit of cheating on very cold days when I move the thermostat up a few degrees. My desire for yet more tender plants is always controlled by the space required for propagation.

My alpine house is by no means ideal. It is a lean-to, so it doesn't permit as much light as true alpines would like, and it backs onto a south wall, so it heats up too much in summer, to the delight of the red spider mites. Between the greenhouse, alpine house, and adjoining potting shed is a little tiled area open to the sky. Thus I have a convenient complex: Potted plants can easily be moved from heated glass to cold glass or to fresh air, with easy access to the potting shed if necessary.

Is it not astonishing how blind one can be? Close to the greenhouse we inherited an ugly wall of concrete blocks heavily disguised with ivy. Fond of ivy as I am, it isn't the most exciting plant in the world, and it would have been just as happy in dryish shade. The sunny side of this wall, a warm corner, would have been perfect for some tender climber, but I couldn't risk removing the ivy and exposing the wall. Years went by before the obvious solution entered my head — to cover the wall on both sides with wooden trellis painted dark green. Now this is an enticing spot, with *Buddleja crispa* on the sunny side, and *Clematis* 'Perle d'Azur', *C.* 'Venosa Violacea', *Ugni molinae* (Zone 9), a myrtle relation with neat evergreen leaves and edible fruits tasting of strawberries, ferns and hellebores in the shade.

When we first arrived, the terrace behind the house was so narrow that we all sat in a row like the queue at the bus station. Our only view was of a large bed of hybrid tea and floribunda roses. I remember announcing that on no account would I ever get rid of them, but I soon became disillusioned with their graceless habit. After weeks of earth moving, the terrace was widened and we built a stone retaining wall, with granite steps leading up to the lawn in the middle. I can never make up my mind which plants merit space on the sunny house walls and flowerbeds beneath, and am always pestering eminent gardeners about what they grow in similar positions. Among the chosen plants of the moment are *Bomarea caldasii, Clematis alpina* 'Frances Rivis', and a variegated myrtle — but ask me next year and I daresay there'll be something different.

I don't like gardening in the front of the house. The garden here is overlooked by passersby, so weeding forays are made early on Sunday mornings. (A vision of me in my gardening clothes could well lower the tone of the neighborhood.) So plants grown here have to satisfy special criteria: They must tolerate poor soil and a north-facing aspect, and they must get by without being fussed over. This means

Plants almost need a letter of reference to qualify for a position in the overcrowded green-house, which is in use throughout the year for propagation.

no staking, no watering, no spraying, and no regular deadheading. The exception to this rule is a large raised bed with some special plants within easy reach of the front door — at the sound of approaching footsteps, I can vanish inside.

Sometimes I find myself sitting down and admiring the garden in a daze. Tunnel vision allows me to notice plants that are looking good or, contrariwise, those plants that look mysteriously unwell, which are often dug up straight away to investigate their roots. But it's only when I observe the garden with a sour, judgmental eye that inspiration arrives: Perhaps that elderly shrub could be replaced — the one I've walked past countless times without actually seeing? Perhaps that marvelous new lungwort should be propagated to make a larger patch? And what about that great vandal of a comfrey? Something must be done.

The most serious gardening I do would seem very strange to an onlooker, for it involves hours of walking round in circles, apparently doing nothing. What I'm doing is forcing myself to evaluate certain areas: criticizing the planting, noting seasonal gaps, and making imaginary moves in my head. Flowering stems are stuck into the soil and plants, still in pots, are plonked down here and there so I can consider the effect. Only during these quiet moments does a good idea suddenly occur. The odd, radical change is contemplated though rarely carried out, such as asking myself what the garden would look like if I got rid of the lawn, moved the main paths, or took out a large apple tree. Gardening is the organization of living, ever-changing organisms, and therefore must be an everlasting, ever-circling process of looking, thinking, and looking again.

Finding The Right Habitat

Y ou come home from the garden center with yet another clematis, rose, fern, hosta, or something with a long Latin name that you *had* to buy, just to see what it was like. Now where are you going to plant it? This momentous decision is fundamental to good gardening, and is particularly crucial for the collector's garden. Don't begin by taking off the label and throwing it away.

One way of organizing the collector's garden is to group together plants of similar habitat. Then when you have two plants, perhaps from opposite ends of the world—such as a Himalayan cyananthus and a Chilean ourisia—growing together in the same cool, moist conditions that both enjoy, they make happy bedfellows. Also, because these plants seem to belong together, the bed *looks* good.

My method of organizing plants is to have an imaginary filing system, using various headings relating to the plant's preferred habitat, such as "sunny well-drained," "sunny moisture-retentive," "moist shade," or "dry shade." (This last category can be the most challenging.) The principal reason for not losing a plant's label is to be able to look up the plant and find out what sort of conditions it enjoys in the wild, and then try to approximate these in the garden. Of course there are numerous subheadings in the main files: Even the shady side of

Raised beds immediately extend the range of garden habitats. Here (beside the greenhouse) they provide the right conditions for sun-loving plants requiring good drainage. The gravel mulch stops weeds from germinating, keeps roots cool in summer, and protects delicate plants from excess winter wet.

Cyclamen hederi-folium grows in dryish shade in a raised bed under the 'Bramley' apple.

a large stone might be just the place for *Ramonda myconi* (Zone 6), a hardy relative of the African violet. And there is no end to the risks one can take with tender plants—*Cyclamen libanoticum* (Zone 9) or the unbelievable turquoise-flowered *Ixia viridiflora* (Zone 9), for example—by tucking them into the sun-baked position at the foot of a south-facing wall. Beside an overflowing water barrel or a dripping tap, or beneath a leaking gutter might be the only possible spot for a moisture lover. If I can't find anything out about a plant, if possible I propagate it immediately in order to be able to grow it in various places. Plants that turn up their noses at the spot I've chosen are moved around until I find a position to their liking.

The greater the range of habitats you can simulate, the better. In my own garden I have done this by building raised beds, lime-free or otherwise, in sun or shade. There are two paved areas: In the Iris Garden sedums, thymes, small campanulas, and *Geranium × riversleaianum* 'Russell Prichard' (Zone 7), this last with rich pink non-stop flowers all summer, can sun themselves on the stone, their roots running cool beneath the slabs, while spaces in the shady paving beneath the 'Bramley' apple provide suitable spots for ferns.

Gravelled areas provide first-class accommodation where the gravel covers the former vegetable garden, or lean conditions with extra good drainage in the drive in front of the house. There's no danger that plantings in gravel or in the gaps between paving stones will look too contrived—self-seeding campanulas, violas, poppies,

foxgloves, and so on will move in so fast, the question will be how many to take out. If some part of your garden has especially poor soil, you could build a raised bed there for that reason alone, as I did. In front of the house an elderly cherry had been robbing the soil for many years. The load of "virgin soil" (as old gardeners call it) that was trundled in had a magical effect on some primroses that had almost faded away.

The Shady Lime-Free Bed

Most gardeners are opportunists to the last. Whatever the local climate, they insist on experimenting with plants on just the other side of the hardiness and suitability line: On heavy clay, they want Mediterranean bulbs; on limy soil, camellias; and naturally, in my part of Dublin, with a thin, limy soil and less than thirty inches of rain per year, nothing has more appeal than acid-loving, woodland plants that demand a cool, moist root run. So, in front of the house, which faces north, I have made a large raised bed supported by low granite walls and filled with lime-free soil. Plants must have exemplary qualifications to be granted space in this bed. They must be desirable in the first place, and I must be quite certain that they wouldn't do just as well somewhere else.

The usual reaction of a gardener with a new lime-free bed to play with is to fill it up with dwarf rhododendrons in one afternoon. The true collector should guard against this, as frustration may ensue. No garden is large enough to accommodate that lot. However, some other members of the Ericaceae are irresistible. *Zenobia pulverulenta* (Zone 5), a suckering shrub now four feet tall, occupies the center of the bed. The leaves are sea green and coated with a fine grayish bloom, to wonderful effect, and the flowers are sparkling white, bell-shaped, and sweetly scented. I remove weak-looking shoots after flowering. Deciduous in Dublin, the leaves of zenobia, I gather, in colder climates turn a beautiful amethyst color in winter.

Mitraria coccinea, listed as hardy only to Zone 10, has never been affected by frost here. What most intrigues me about this plant is that it is a Chilean member of the Gesneriaceae, and thus a cousin of the African violet. (I am still searching for some family likeness.) Although it has been called a "straggling subshrub"—a rude description for a smart, well-behaved plant—it is easily coaxed into being a climber. (Here it grows seven feet high against the house wall.) It has shining evergreen leaves and tubular, brilliant red flowers in late summer, about one inch long and waxy to the touch. My plant is in deep shade. The tips of the outer branches are trimmed in spring; the plant is easily propagated by Irishman's cuttings. (These cuttings, explained E. A. Bowles, are "newly rooted portions, round the old plants. Of course, if you are taking off a few to give to a visitor from the Emerald Isle, you must be careful to speak of Dutchman's cuttings instead, or take the risk of adding one more insult to the distressful country.")

Deinanthe caerulea (Zone 6) is a Chinese herbaceous perennial, about two feet tall, related to the hydrangeas, discovered and introduced by the renowned Irish plant collector Augustine Henry (more about him later). The nodding flowers are odd to touch, both cool and full of body, and an extraordinary color, the kind of retiring murky blue that can only dwell in the shade. The slate-blue stamens are exquisite against the clair-de-lune petals, but the whole ensemble is impossible to capture on film. Perhaps the consequent lack of publicity is the reason for its rarity. In dry summers the bold, crinkly, coarse-textured leaves are subject to mildew. The white-flowered Japanese *Deinanthe bifida* (Zone 6) is similar, somewhat taller, and not quite so rare, though nearly as beautiful. Propagate both by division, should you feel inclined. I don't. My bones tell me deinanthes would hate to be disturbed.

Anemonopsis macrophylla (Zone 4), also from Japan, has demure little nodding flowers with rounded, creamy-white waxy petals shading to violet at the edges, the sort of color found only on a very expensive dress. It is a lovely thing, with lustrous, dark green foliage. This is usually marred at flowering time in Dublin by cold winds that turn the leaves yellow green. It comes easily from seed. Division is also recommended, but I've never tried.

Petals with a waxen feel seem to belong in the shade. The pendant, bell-shaped rosy-red flowers, flared at the rim, of *Philesia magellanica* (Zone 9), a small shrubby member of the lily family from Chile, are sensationally cool and fleshy. They are

Primula *'Peter Klein'*, growing in the shady, lime-free bed, is one of the most reliable, long-lived primroses in the garden.

remarkably large (about two inches long) for the size of the plant. For the first few years all you have is leathery, dark evergreen leaves, with paler, blue-green reverses. The flexible stems (to fifteen inches or so) move around underground, the shoots coming up at random. Apparently, philesia starts to flower better when the roots are restricted. A good way to achieve this might be to grow it in a stone trough, kept in the shade and well watered. Propagate it by Irishman's cuttings.

Jeffersonia dubia (Zone 5) is an herbaceous member of the barberry family, or Berberidaceae, with romantic origins: It comes from the forests of Manchuria and eastern Siberia and was named in honor of Thomas Jefferson. I find especially fascinating that such an exquisite small plant (it grows to about one foot), which dares to produce its ethereal lavender flowers and heavenly, purple-flushed leaves in the biting winds of March, should be related to *Berberis buxifolia*. (This latter is the nasty, spiny, leg-scratching shrub I met with only too often in the foothills of the Andes in Chile.) The white-flowered, North American species, *J. diphylla* (Zone 5), is a new acquisition.

The really classy primroses get into this bed, not because they need lime-free soil, but because they fade away elsewhere. The green primrose, *Primula vulgaris* 'Viridis' (Zone 4), is one such. Obtaining this primrose poses a unique problem for the collector: They say the fairies will get you

Meconopsis ×shel-
donii *'Slieve Donard'*,
the finest of all the blue
poppies, bears the name
of an Irish mountain.

if you buy it; but it is equally bad luck to be given it. I gather the only safe way to get your hands on it is to steal it. Several attempts have been made to try the old Irish double polyanthus 'Our Pat' in other parts of the garden, but it refuses to survive unless in this bed. This has double, deep plum-colored, yellow-eyed flowers and purple-flushed leaves. *Primula* 'Peter Klein', a hybrid between *P. clarkei* (Zone 7; sweet, small, rose-pink, liable to die) and *P. rosea* (Zone 6; more vigorous, moisture-loving) seems reliable, insofar as any primula is here. The young foliage is bronze, an attractive foil for the shocking pink, early spring flowers.

After I read a description of *Paris polyphylla* (Zone 6) by Graham Thomas in his *Perennial Garden Plants*, I knew that this curious member of the Liliaceae (or Trilliaceae, depending on which authority you prefer) was a plant I had to have. Smooth stems, about two feet tall, support a symmetrical ruff of leaves. To describe the flowers correctly is to get into a fierce botanical muddle, for what appear to be green petals are in fact sepals, whereas the petals look like the stamens. These are extremely long, thin, and like the legs of an upside-down spider. In the middle is a large, shiny, maroon knob, which is in fact the stigma. Ever determined to encourage larger flowers (if such you could call them), I moved *Paris* several times to richer, more humusy soil. I then met it growing in a Himalayan glade, and found it looked no better in the wild. (It is now known as *Daiswa polyphylla* from the local Nepalese name for the plant.) It is easy, though slow, from seed.

Meconopsis betonicifolia (Zone 4) is the blue poppy. A short-lived perennial, easy from seed, it requires cool conditions and the nearest you can get to Himalayan mist—in the wild, the plants are constantly saturated in droplets of moisture. The toothed leaves are grayish green and slightly hairy. The color of the flowers can be anything between heavenly sky blue and a wishy-washy mauve. You'd be perfectly happy with *M. betonicifolia*, provided you'd never seen *M. ×sheldonii* 'Slieve Donard' (Zone 6). This is a dream of a plant, with flowers of a blue so brilliant you will immediately dig up *M. betonicifolia* and give it away, as I did. Now I only grow the form *M. betonicifolia* 'Alba'—rather nice, with no variation in the white of the tissue-paperlike petals, and it conveniently seeds itself.

M. ×sheldonii 'Slieve Donard' gives a fair account of itself in this shady, lime-free bed. A true perennial, it is divided every two years in early autumn, and replanted with a large amount of well-rotted cow manure (two to three buckets per square yard) worked into the planting area. In colder areas it would be better to divide it in spring. There's never much root on these plants at the best of times, so don't pull the plants into very small sections. It's sterile, and so cannot be grown from seed.

Dianella tasmanica (Zone 9) has grasslike, shiny, evergreen leaves around three feet tall and small, pale blue flowers followed by bright blue, polished fruits. It wouldn't thrive anywhere until it was moved to this exclusive bed, whereupon it set off by means of underground shoots. It came up in the middle of the bloodroot, tied its roots in knots

around the trilliums, and started to annex the toad lilies before I decided it would have to go. A large section of the bed had to be dug up and replanted.

Gravel

Don't you think that the typical small front garden, with its minuscule patch of lawn and an occasional shrub, would be much better turned into a gravel garden? It would be soothing to look at and easy to maintain; there wouldn't be any grass to mow; and all the planting would be unified by the top dressing of pebbles. If my plot were very small, that's exactly what I'd do. Moreover, a remarkable range of plants, including ferns and shade lovers, relish the cool soil under a mulch of washed pebbles or pea gravel.

The idea of laying a large sheet of black plastic on the site before spreading the gravel is not so clever as it seems. Agreed, weeds have no chance whatsoever; but the small stones invariably shift, cluster in hollows, and expose ugly patches of plastic, thus spoiling the pleasant illusion that the garden is actually located on a seam of gravel. Gravel is always easy to weed, but needs topping up regularly.

We usually think of a mulch of small stones only for raised, sunny, well-drained alpine beds. But there is no reason why you cannot have a rich, vegetable soil, full of humus, under the gravel for plants that need it. Here, in part shade, the brittle bladder fern (*Cystopteris fragilis;* Zone 2), various crested and frilly-leaved forms of the

hart's-tongue fern (*Asplenium scolopendrium;* Zone 5) and the maidenhair spleenwort (*Asplenium trichomanes;* Zone 2) have been content for years. Choose small-stoned gravel—larger stones are uncomfortable to walk on and make an irritating scrunch as you go.

There are some plants that for the sake of their health must be consigned to starvation corner. If you give the perennial wallflower, *Erysimum* 'Bowles' Mauve' (Zone 6) or the old, double yellow wallflower 'Harpur Crewe' (Zone 6) too rich a soil, they become gross and liable to keel over—wallflowers have little root at the best of times. These two are growing in the gravel drive in front of the house in full sun, with only a handful or two of soil mixed with the gravel in their planting holes.

The end of the line for certain plants is the drive, where they are given their last chance to behave themselves. The two-foot-high *Rubus illecebrosus* (Zone 5) is such a one, with white flowers and pinnate prickly leaves. The lean cuisine on the drive certainly curbs its invasive temperament. It is an amusing plant on account of its large, red, enticing fruits, which look like a cross between a strawberry and a large, juicy raspberry. But it tastes of nothing much at all—even the blackbirds look disappointed after trying one. The rose-root, *Rhodiola rosea* (Zone 3), also known as *Sedum rosea*, an inviting plant in spring when stems of glaucous leaves terminate in rosy-mauve flower buds, is also grown in the gravel drive in the hope that vine weevils (which adore the fleshy roots) would never think of looking for it there.

The best-appointed graveled area is at the base of a sundial encircled by the large raised bed. The soil here is good, as it is the original site of the vegetable garden. *Geum montanum* (Zone 6), the alpine avens, often treated as the poor relation among geums, is a thoroughly nice plant. It has golden yellow flowers on eight-inch stems in spring, followed by large, feathery, silvery seedheads that linger for ages. My clump, which has been divided only twice in eighteen years, still thrives in the same spot. *Allium beesianum* (Zone 6) growing nearby has refreshing bell-shaped Wedgwood blue flowers with deeper central veins in August.

Geranium sinense (Zone 6), from southwestern China, also grows in the gravel. Strictly speaking, I should listen to my own advice and move it to a less prominent position. This is an intriguing but not especially showy geranium, with nectar that is madly attractive to wasps and hoverflies. Wicked black-and-yellow-striped insects and sinister, velvety black reflexed flowers seem to go together. The flowers appear in late summer on two-foot stems.

Ireland is an area of such low light intensity that the sunniest possible position must be chosen for pinks (*Dianthus* cultivars; Zone 4). Mine are all propagated just after flowering, by cuttings firmed into a finger-deep, sand-lined trench outside and watered often during the critical first few weeks. At the cutting stage, despite elaborate labeling, they are always getting muddled up. I never dare discard the old colony of plants until the young lot have bloomed the following year, in case one of the collection gets lost. As a result, I have pinks in rather too many places, including this prime spot in the gravel around the sundial. In winter, watch out for parties of slugs making merry under the mounds of blue-gray foliage. The most sensational dianthus here is one that originated in Ireland named 'Chomley Farran', a sport of a crimson border carnation. The flowers are a gorgeous combination of mulberry purple and cherry pink, with all the opulence of an Elizabethan jester's jacket. It is constantly being propagated as I'm terrified of losing this, the cream of my collection.

The Terrace

I do so envy the beginner gardener. There are no "buts" when you are just starting: "*But* this plant hates lime." "*But* it's tender." "*But* it'll get too big." Trying one of This, ten of That, and two dozen of The Other, you plant away in glorious ignorance. Wonderful fun. But now, jaded by experience, I can read through catalogs filled with goodies and manage to resist the lot. A long-established garden such as this is bound to be static, with too many long-loved plants that I cannot even think about disturbing.

The terrace, facing due south and backed by the sunny wall of the house, is my only playground, where I can experiment with tender plants and plan something new for each year. After their brilliant but ephemeral summer display, salpiglossis, nicotianas, and petunias, or whatever annual is the fancy of the moment, can be rushed to the com-

OVERLEAF

The soil in the pots on the terrace is renewed often—annuals always get fresh soil. At the moment (the recipe is always changing) I'm using a mix of two buckets peat-based potting mixture, one bucket home-made garden compost, and half a bucket of coarse grit plus slow-release fertilizer.

post heap without a qualm. And I can rearrange the pots every day if I feel like it.

I have terra-cotta pots for box balls, box standards (slow to mature from cuttings taken six years ago), box cones, and two box soufflés. I made the soufflés by taking two shallow terra-cotta pots and filling them to within four inches of the rim with soil (not quite as full as usual). These were closely planted with dwarf box all over. Clipped tightly into shallow domes that rise no more than three inches in the center, these bright green vegetable puddings come into their own in winter.

An extra big terra-cotta pot stands sentinel at each corner of the terrace. Each has a permanent resident shrub. One contains lime-free soil and *Hydrangea macrophylla* (Zone 5), in an effort to have a blue hydrangea. (My soil is alkaline, so they're always pink in the open ground.) The other pot is home for *Fuchsia magellanica* 'Versicolor' (Zone 7), with coppery pink young foliage that matures to silvery gray-green, a perfect complement to the terra-cotta of the pot. For company, the fuchsia has double white argyranthemums, mauve and pink verbenas, white petunias, and silver helichrysums for summer; blue pansies and a staggered display of tulips for spring. Nothing original about that, you might say. This summer I'm trying a deep apricot form of *Alonsoa warscewiczii* and *Pelargonium* 'Frank Headley'. This pelargonium resists wet Irish summers better than most, and its deep salmon flowers are in gentle accord with both the pot and the alonsoa.

At the foot of the house wall is a large and ever-changing congregation of potted plants. Having always believed in centralized mess, with chaos in one place only (in the house this is the kitchen table), I think you can assemble a miscellany of pots, provided they are grouped all together. The group itself then acts as a single element in the overall design. An extra illusion of order is imposed by two larger pots, in which I try to restrict myself to just one type of plant—forget-me-nots for spring and petunias for summer.

Some long-resident pot plants are yuccas, sempervivums, echeverias, and the giant reed, *Arundo donax* 'Variegata' (the species is listed as Zone 6 but the variegated form is more tender), with stems bearing blue-green leaves smartly striped in white. There are several different francoas (in the wild I saw some growing in the spray of a waterfall in Chile), including *Francoa ramosa* (Zone 7), the bridal wreath, which had a seal of approval as a pot plant from Miss Jekyll: "the plant knows what is expected of it and intends to fulfill its settled duty and purpose, namely, that of being a graceful and beautiful ornament." She obviously liked a plant that knew how to behave. Francoas have basal rosettes of dark evergreen, slightly shiny, deeply lobed leaves and elegant wands of little white, pink, or pale purple flowers. And I could never be without lemon-scented verbena, *Aloysia triphylla* (Zone 8), which has panicles of boring flowers and nondescript leaves, redeemed by a divine scent when the leaves are crushed, like the fragrance of those expensive, lemon-shaped soaps that come in special wooden boxes.

There are also three raised beds on the terrace. On the left, slightly shaded by an old pear tree, is

The flowers of the pineapple lily (Eucomis bicolor) emit a whiff of long-boiled cabbage. Happily, flowering doesn't last long and the seed heads remain decorative for months.

a bed for acid-loving plants. Hanging over the edge is an obscure, prostrate conifer for the collector, *Microcachrys tetragona* (Zone 8), a member of the Podocarpaceae from Tasmania, where it creeps over the rocks. It has sweet little female cones, which mature to a translucent bright orange red. This is still recovering from being sat on by a large Dutchman, a horrible shock for such a choice little thing. Nearby is *Ribes laurifolium* (Zone 6), a refined evergreen currant, slow-growing to four feet, with dense clusters of lime green flowers in late winter, and a patch of *Primula megaseifolia* (Zone 7), which produces magenta-

rose flowers with white-rimmed yellow eyes; rare, but not madly exciting, except that it blooms in winter during mild periods. *Billardiera longiflora* (Zone 8), a twiner from Tasmania, with small pale yellow-green bells followed by super glossy, bright blue berries, has seeded itself into the middle of a dwarf rhododendron, but looks so good I'm letting it be. The cute Australian violet, *Viola hederacea* (Zone 8), runs about all over this bed.

The nomadic plant population in the raised bed in the center includes, as I write, *Bomarea caldasii* (Zone 9), a South American climbing relation of alstroemeria. This is rather special, but, resentful of the lack of Irish sun, it rarely deigns to produce more than one or two exotic umbels of glowing orange tubular flowers. It has nevertheless twined its way fifteen feet up the wall—you can't even get close to examine the flowers' spotted interiors.

At its feet is a group of pineapple lilies, *Eucomis bicolor* (Zone 8), South African summer-flowering bulbs. I suspect they're hardier than people think. I've got some growing in the open garden and "there's not a bother on them," as they say. Stout stems, speckled in maroon, support cylindrical spikes of starry light green flowers, topped with a tidy tuffet of shiny leaves. The whole effect is of a pineapple, except that the flowers emit a whiff of long-boiled cabbage; happily flowering doesn't last long, and as they look almost exactly the same whether in flower or seed, they remain decorative way into autumn.

A prostrate form of *Coronilla valentina* (Zone 9) drapes itself over the edge of this bed. I saw this plant peeping out of heavy snow in the High Atlas mountains of Morocco, so I don't believe the recommended Zone 9. It has pretty little blue-green leaves and golden clusters of scented pea flowers all through winter and spring. It can spread to four feet. The tender *C. valentina* 'Citrina' produces pale lemon flowers for months in a pot in the greenhouse. Both are easy from cuttings.

A longtime resident of the largest raised bed is *Clematis alpina* 'Frances Rivis', an easy, nonwilting clematis, abundantly decked in sky-blue flowers with creamy white centers in spring. It doesn't have to occupy such a choice, sunny position, but I

haven't the heart to remove it, so good does it look entwined with nearby *Luma apiculata* 'Glanleam Gold'. This may still be a *Myrtus*—again the botanists are at loggerheads about what its name should be. The variegation of 'Glanleam Gold' is more Jersey cream than gold; it was found in Ireland during the 1960s. Deep coral *Lathyrus rotundifolius* (Zone 6), the Persian everlasting pea, seeds itself around, and *Malva sylvestris* 'Primley Blue' (Zone 5), a lovely thing and long-lived for the mallow family, tumbles over the edge. Depending on the whim of the moment, all manner of plants might be found in this bed, but *Salvia* 'Indigo Spires' (Zone 5), *S. cacaliifolia* (Zone 9), *Melianthus major*, and cannas are regulars.

Lord Anson's blue pea (*Lathyrus nervosus*; Zone 8) grows (with some reluctance), in a Victorian cast-iron urn. In 1744, during a four-year round-the-world voyage, Lord Anson put into Cape Horn and "these Peas were a great relief to the sailors," who were starved of fresh food, as Christopher Brickell and Fay Sharman write in *The Vanishing Garden*. Seeds were brought home to the family seat, Shugborough, in Staffordshire, by Lord Anson's cook. The leaves are pale gray-green, and strangely rigid to the touch. The flowers are soft blue with a hint of mauve, and large for the size of the plant. Sometimes described as fragrant, this could only have been written by somebody who'd never sat downwind of *Lathyrus nervosus* on a warm day; to my nose the plant has a carcinogenic odor of petrol and weedkiller combined.

Thoughts About Color

F or me, emphatically, the plant always comes first. Every effort should be made to grow it well. Then comes a problem of delicious complication: How to place it so that it not only looks good in itself, but also complements its neighbors. So, all else being equal, I try to plant with color in mind. But somebody who loves plants for their individual beauty cannot think for long on the broad spectrum.

Designers are capable of ordering plants by the hundred, whereas a collector grudges the space used up by planting more than one specimen. Repetition of groups of the same plant will give instant coherence to a random planting. A semblance of order is further provided by the use of restraint (a word not normally found in the collector's vocabulary) in the form of planting generous large patches of certain plants, particularly low-growing foliage plants that look good throughout the season. So, in the main borders, I have practiced a little self-control by planting several groups of dwarf purple-leafed barberry, catmint, *Artemisia* 'Powis Castle' (Zone 6), *Heuchera micrantha* 'Palace Purple' (Zone 5), and *Anaphalis triplinervis* (Zone 5). Ordinary plants are just what you want here; even a wide pool of *Alchemilla mollis* (Zone 3) would refresh the eye after examining a throng of rarities, each vying for attention. Even better if this pool is echoed by another further along the border.

PRECEDING

OVERLEAF

The Blue Border.
Purists will say that
you shouldn't mix pure
blue with mauve-blue.
I don't care—I adore
blue flowers. My
method is to make a
glorious muddle of all
the different blues.

How often does one read that a garden is "a riot of color"? An all-too-vivid scene presents itself, in which a serious disturbance appears to be taking place: the scarlet flowers fighting the shocking pinks, the bright oranges indulging in wild revelry behind the hedge, loud clashes as the magentas join the fray and a few poor whites cower under a bush. What a disorderly display.

For fifteen years I was quite unaware of the most excruciating clashes; I was far too busy being captivated by the sight of yet another new plant. Then, at last, having always loved plants for themselves alone, I started to wonder how to organize the garden so as to present a tranquil scene of order rather than one of chaos. Thus began the blue border.

The Blue Border

Should someone (with a disapproving wave of the color wheel) attempt to explain, yet again, Jekyllian theory on matters of color, I shall take no notice. I adore blue flowers; they are scarce enough at the best of times. My method is to mix all shades together, making a glorious muddle of different blues, never mind whether they are turquoise, sapphire, or lapis lazuli. Purists will say that you shouldn't mix pure blues with mauve- or violet-blue, but the loveliest effects can be made by breaking the rules. Indeed, in this part of the garden it is hard to see where the blue stops and the mauve begins,

Goat's rue (Galega officinalis), essential in the Blue Border for taking over as the delphiniums fade, is divided every second year to keep the clumps vigorous.

shading to mauve and violet in the shadow, illuminated here and there by some silvery mounds of artemisias.

Delphiniums (Zone 3) are trouble. They need watering. They need frequent division and extra-rich soil. They need constant protection against slugs and often need spraying against mildew. They may need to have their surplus shoots thinned in spring. And you almost need a doctorate in delphinium staking to get that right—if the string is too loose, the stems snap; too tight, ditto. But when they bloom, I am recompensed for all the bother by their glorious blue spires, which bring to mind the grand old herbaceous borders you see in fading photographs and Edwardian watercolors. All my delphiniums have lost their names, so I call each different one after the gardener who gave me the original division. As for "pink" delphiniums, to me this seems a contradiction in terms. But I might be persuaded to entertain a good white.

Larkspurs (*Consolida* cultivars) self-sow with abandon, presenting slender spikes in various shades of blue, just when their cousins, the larger delphiniums, are going over. The hazy blue of love-in-a-mist (*Nigella damascena*) appears here and there at the border front, each flower surrounded by a lacy ruff of finely cut foliage. Love-in-a-mist's other name is devil-in-a-bush, because the inflated seed pods have horns like archetypal devils. Should your climate permit, both these annuals make stronger plants when autumn-sown and left undisturbed; just thin them out as necessary in spring.

Goat's rue, *Galega officinalis* (Zone 4), was a familiar plant in Edwardian borders but seemed to go out of fashion as this century matured, lost in the multitude of new arrivals on the perennial scene. Easy, long-flowering, so reliable and so pretty—a mauvy lilac cloud—it quickly becomes indispensable.

In the hiatus as the first flush of delphiniums goes over, I don't know what I'd do without three large groups of goat's rue. A vigorous perennial to four feet, this member of the pea family has branching heads packed with little sweet-pea flowers and light green, featherlike leaves. There are several cultivars, including the white 'Alba'. Early summer-flowering *Galega orientalis* (Zone 6) from the Caucasus has super bright blue flowers with a hint of violet. It can be invasive, but I'm hopeful that the nearby roots of a long-established patch of Japanese anemones might dampen its ardor.

Monkshoods are essential follow-on plants to the delphiniums. In the blue border they are represented by *Aconitum* × *cammarum* 'Bicolor', with branching inflorescence of nodding, hooded, two-tone blue-and-white flowers on four-foot stems, and 'Bressingham Spire', not so tall, with violet-blue flowers. Beautiful as they are, you'd almost know by the threatening look of the helmeted flowers that these plants are deadly poisonous; many's the story about how Victorian gardeners perished because they mistook monkshood tubers for Jerusalem artichokes. Monkshoods require little staking. Give them a fertile soil, not too dry; they will tolerate part shade. Divide them in autumn if necessary.

In the Blue Border Clematis ✕ durandii is treated as an herbaceous plant. Its trailing stems are excellent for draping over the fading leaves of Oriental poppies or spring bulbs.

You probably know it only as a bedding plant, but here *Salvia patens* (Zone 8) behaves as a perennial, growing to two feet at the border front. The velvety flowers are such a vivid pure blue that their color dominates all paler blues nearby (including its cultivar 'Cambridge Blue'), especially those with a mauvy hue.

In late summer the ongoing confrontation between collector and maker of garden pictures temporarily subsides, and space is allowed for some decent groups of *Aster ✕ frikartii* 'Mönch' and *Aster thomsonii* 'Nanus'. These two mauvy-blue daisies, both bountiful of flower, hold court

for many weeks with an ever-changing retinue that includes *Clematis ✕ durandii*, *Buddleja davidii* 'Nanho Blue', catmint, blue verbenas, stokesia, agapanthus, echinops, eryngium, violas, *Salvia* 'Indigo Spires', *S. uliginosa*, and campanulas—from towering clumps of milky blue *C. lactiflora* to the peach-leaved bellflower, *C. persicifolia*.

So far we've discussed only blue flowers, but there are also swags of gray foliage and bouquets of white flowers in the blue border—white penstemons, white agapanthus, and airy sprays of gypsophila, for example. Foliage accents are provided by teasels (*Dipsacus fullonum*; Zone 3), and

Violas in the Blue Border, including the best of the lot, the perennial Viola cornuta *(pale lilac, at right). All pansies and violas are deadheaded almost daily throughout the summer.*

a Queen Anne's lace lookalike called *Selinum wallichianum* (Zone 6), formerly *S. tenuifolium*, perhaps the most beautiful of all cow parsleys, with a filigree of fresh green fernlike leaves and flowers quite superior to the wild plant of Irish hedgerows. There is also quite a lot of mauve, with plants such as *Penstemon* 'Alice Hindley' and *P.* 'Sour Grapes'. (I don't know if this latter is the true plant, there are so many pretenders about.)

Few visitors notice *Corokia cotoneaster* (Zone 8), the wire netting bush from New Zealand. It has silvery young growth, tortuously interlaced branches going in all directions, and small, oval, silver-green leaves. With no obvious leading shoot and a cagelike tangle of branches, it has been suggested that *C. cotoneaster* evolved like this to protect the tender leader from grazing moas, a giant extinct bird. You wouldn't think it pretty, neither by its common name nor this description, but it forms a pleasant bulge of smoky gray about six feet tall, a gentle foil for the blue of delphiniums and aconitums. Background shrubs must be amenable to the gardener's whim, so this is lightly pruned to size in spring.

Hebe speciosa 'Tricolor' (Zone 7) grows nearby. The oval, evergreen leaves are on the borderline between being an appropriate choice for a pastel color scheme and being a smidgen too flashy— pale green edged with cream and tinted at the edges with purple-pink. The late-summer flowers are reddish-magenta. This hebe is kept to about four feet by regular spring pruning. From the moment I decided that I didn't really care whether it died or not in a hard winter (I would, of course, have replaced it with a young plant from another spot in the garden), this specimen has apparently become immune to frost.

The Red Border

One day somebody will write a complicated thesis on why women dislike strong colors in the garden. Most take exception to red and strong yellow, while orange is considered impossible. It seems that they would prefer to drift around in a haze of sweet pea colors, accompanied by mounds of lavender and plants with silver leaves.

The red border came about for two reasons. The first was *Lychnis chalcedonica* (Zone 4), the Maltese cross. Wherever I put it, the worse it looked—the scarlet of its flowers dazzled everything else into oblivion. I gave it away. But it's a sad state of affairs if a fine old garden plant has to go because the right place cannot be found. Secondly, I visited Mount Stewart, the National Trust garden in Northern Ireland, one of those rare gardens with good plants as well as good

design. There, laid out before me, was the solution, so simple you'd have to be color blind not to see and understand.

The great parterre, to the south of the house, is divided into two clear sections: to the left are all the strong colors—red, orange, bright yellow; to the right, the pastel shades—pink, pale blue, mauve, and light yellow. Suddenly everything made sense. After fifteen years of enjoying plants just for themselves, I wanted to make garden pictures as well. Back home I began a total reorganization of color. This involved umpteen plant moves, many of them taking place in summer so I could see what the colors were.

I began to collect foliage plants to use as background to all the different reds. The collector's attitude of never having more than one specimen had to be staunched, so some plants are used repetitively in the red border, such as dwarf red barberry (*Berberis thunbergii* 'Atropurpurea Nana'; Zone 4), *Heuchera micrantha* 'Palace Purple' (Zone 5), and *Euphorbia dulcis* 'Chameleon' (Zone 6). This last is herbaceous, with rich rosy-purple leaves. It looks good most of the year, so late is it to bed and so early to rise. Nice seedlings in various shades of purple turn up, but if you want to preserve the true plant, propagate it by division or cuttings. I'm told cuttings root at any time of year, but I've found basal spring cuttings best.

A form of cow parsley or Queen Anne's lace, *Anthriscus sylvestris* 'Ravenswing' (Zone 6) has leaves that emerge green and change to purple black; the flowers are creamy white. *Cimicifuga*

Rodgersia pinnata 'Superba' (left) has wonderfully textured leaves that keep their bronze flush throughout the season. Here, it's growing with an apricot kniphofia and self-seeding double white feverfew (Tanacetum parthenium 'White Bonnet').

PRECEDING

OVERLEAF

Looking toward the Red Border from the terrace, with angel's fishing rod (Dierama pulcherrimum) arching over the sphinx on the right.

simplex Atropurpurea Group is a distinguished plant, with sultry deep purple leaves and sweetly scented bottle-brush flowers on four- to five-foot stems. It appreciates rich, moist soil, is comparatively slow to increase, and has been divided only twice in eleven years. (This was done out of greed; it didn't actually need dividing).

Heuchera 'Pewter Moon' (Zone 5), a recent addition, has prettily veined and marbled leaves in matte silver, the undersides washed in mauve. Whereas a singleton is charming, I can't wait to have a group. No sooner than a new plant starts to bulk up, it is in danger of being hauled out of the ground and divided.

Cercis canadensis 'Forest Pansy' (Zone 4), a large shrub or small tree, is still on trial. The leaves are satiny, heart-shaped, crimson, and breathtaking as the evening sun shines through them. I have read that this plant can be stooled by hard pruning in spring, so I'm not worried if it suffers from spring die-back.

Mahonia × *wagneri* 'Moseri' (Zone 7) is rather good, with bronze-salmon young leaves, later turning to green on thirty-inch stems. It suckers in all directions once established. Other foliage plants here include a dwarf purple-leaved New Zealand flax, bronze-leaved ajuga, red-leaved spinach and beetroot, *Penstemon digitalis* 'Husker's Red' (Zone 3), and *Uncinia rubra* (Zone 8). One doesn't often think of roses as foliage plants, but the red flush of their young leaves tones nicely in spring with purple tulips, crimson winter pansies, and double red primroses.

Two ordinary background shrubs in this bed are a purple form of the smoke bush, *Cotinus coggygria* (Zone 5), and *Rosa glauca* (once called *R. rubrifolia;* Zone 4), a foliage plant *par excellence* with rosy-mauve glaucous leaves, pale pink flowers like little Tudor roses, and a copious supply of red hips in autumn. Both are liable to be pruned at whim. The rose, if cut almost to ground level in spring, will produce wands of much larger leaves, a lovely compensation for the lack of flower. I adore this plant, and consider it one of the ten best plants of all. It is just as pretty in shade, when the leaves assume an even bluer hue. With regard to the cotinus, it would be more subtle to use a cultivar with leaves not quite so dense a purple, but I've yet to acquire one.

I once knew a gardening poseur who used to sit down to lunch, his secateurs, clean and freshly oiled, laid beside his knife and fork. Afterwards, accompanied by his entourage on the garden tour, each shrub received a snip with the secateurs, regardless of whether it needed it or not. No doubt the onlookers were impressed. I'm all for breaking the rules, but I think it is important to find out which shrubs one can take liberties with—the rose and the smoke bush above willingly submit to such cavalier treatment.

Now for the flowers: *Dahlia* 'Bishop of Llandaff' is a stunningly good plant—the metallic dark bronze-purple foliage is infinitely better than the usual cabbagey dahlia leaves, and the single bright red flowers are the height of refinement. But as the flowers age, a hint of vulgarity

'Bishop of Llandaff' is the star of the Red Border and also a potentate in the dahlia tribe, on account of its superb bronze foliage.

Kniphofia thomsonii *var.* snowdenii *is easily distinguished from other red-hot pokers by its widely spaced florets and the fact that it produces a long succession of flowers.*

creeps in, so they are often deadheaded before their time. *Dahlia* 'Bednall Beauty' is a similar, much smaller version, the flowers slightly more crimson than scarlet. Very nice.

Roses here include 'Alexander', a ferocious vermilion, but I think there's enough bronze foliage around to cope with it, 'Frensham', a softer red, gentle on the eye; and 'Marlena'—I don't like the form of the flowers, but they are a nice shade of red. 'Bengal Rose', a rare and not very hardy rose that seems to be close to the wild *Rosa chinensis*, has such pretty single floppy-petaled flowers that I had to try it here, but it may prove too tender for such an open position.

This year *Knautia macedonica* (Zone 6) had its first flower in February and its last in November. The flowers, like little purple-red pincushions, require some support. *Kniphofia* 'Samuel's Sensation' (Zone 7) is a flamboyant poker with tall bright carmine flowers, but *K. thomsonii* var. *snowdenii* (Zone 8), distinguished by its curved florets widely spaced on the stem, is soft orange.

Penstemon 'Chester Scarlet' and 'Burgundy' (Zone 9) are important for continuity of color: Each autumn emergency cuttings are taken, but I can never bear to replace the old plants in spring. *Crocosmia* 'Lucifer' (Zone 6), *C.* 'Carmin Brilliant',

and *C.* 'Mrs. Morrison' (both Zone 7) are divided every second year. Small frontal plants include *Verbena* × *hybrida* 'Lawrence Johnston' (Zone 9), red antirrhinums, and nicotiana.

Iris chrysographes 'Inshriach' (Zone 6), a small black velvet iris, was once nearly lost through dividing it in late summer (apparently the correct time is spring). As black as you'll get (more so than 'Black Knight'), it looks good in the red border, while *Baptisia australis* (Zone 4) and *Gentiana asclepiadea* (Zone 5), two good blues, have to remain despite their color. Neither can be transplanted; when the chips are down, plants come before fancy color schemes.

Lastly, I should mention the rare *Hemerocallis fulva* 'Kwanso Variegata' (Zone 4). Imported from Japan in the 1860s, this has double soft orange flowers, with bronzy-red shading. The leaves, smartly silver-striped, are decorative from the moment they come up. 'Kwanso Variegata' sat and looked at me for years before there was enough of it to divide.

The challenge of arranging this border is endlessly fascinating, perhaps because there's no chance whatsoever of getting it right—the more I think about it the more complicated it becomes. Parts of the border work quite well, sometimes, but never the whole thing all at once.

The Plants

Agapanthus

The story about the elderly lady in the west of Ireland who put up a notice saying "Beware of the Agapanthus" may well be apocryphal, but it's worth repeating nonetheless. Apparently she was annoyed by uninvited guests helping themselves to plants. The notice had the desired effect—*agapanthus* sounds more like the name of a vicious dinosaur than of a beautiful perennial African lily, although in fact it comes from the Greek *agapē*, love, and *anthos*, flower.

In the golden afternoons before World War I, no Edwardian terrace was complete without its row of wooden tubs filled with blue African lilies. In the autumn, the plant, tub and all, would be trundled under glass for winter. *Agapanthus* is a confusing genus, and this is reflected in its tortuous nomenclature. Most writers support the contention that *A. africanus* was the species widely grown at this time, but that name is perhaps not correct.

Those species with wide, shining, evergreen leaves are liable to be tender; the deciduous species are generally hardier. The Headbourne hybrids, bred by Lewis Palmer during the 1950s and 1960s, are probably the most reliable.

"Most species…thrive when overcrowded," says *The New Royal Horticultural Society Dictionary of Gardening*. I don't agree—if they aren't divided here every

Safe from careless feet, dwarf agapanthus in variety grow on the raised bed in the Sundial Garden; the silver-leaved plant is the superb Celmisia semicordata *'David Shackleton'.*

three years or so, few flowers are produced. Division is a major operation, for disentangling the congested, fleshy roots is heavy work. They usually have to be chopped up with a kitchen knife.

All the different blues, from pale powder to intense deep blue, introduce invaluable cool tones to soften the strident yellows of late summer. In the case of white agapanthus, I operate a one-person selection committee. I used to have a floppy, not very floriferous clone that I discarded in favor of a superb, compact, late-flowering plant with ivory buds flushed with palest green, opening to white flowers with dark stamens. (Both were bought at plant sales and are hence anonymous.)

The smaller cultivars, 'Midnight Blue', 'Lilliput' (dark blue), and 'Lady Moore' (rare, white, late flowering) are grown on the largest raised bed near the celmisias (see page 93), forming a nice patch of color among mainly spring-flowering plants. Even their autumn seed-heads are decorative on a minor scale.

One agapanthian temptation I mistakenly fell for is the double *Agapanthus praecox* 'Flore Pleno'. It rarely bloomed, and the few miserable flowers were supported by stubby, unattractive flower stalks. *Agapanthus praecox* 'Variegatus', on the other hand, has such smart cream and green stripes that it is worth waiting for the odd flower. Well deserving of its exclusive spot in the greenhouse, it is also a useful summer foliage plant outside.

For me, the species to tickle the palate of the jaded collector has to be *Agapanthus inapertus*. With slender, trumpet-shaped, pendulous flow-ers, it is easily distinguished from other species—you can recognize it even from a distance by the shape of the flowerheads. Unpoetic as it sounds, these are best described as in the shape of a mop, supported on erect stems; other agapanthus have stems that lean toward the sun. There are several different blue forms, but the most thrilling of all has deep violet flowers with an almost plumlike bloom on the petals. It caused much anxiety this year, when the warm spring encouraged it to sprout too soon and the crown was turned to mush by late frost. However, the roots were still firm and it is recovering in a pot—a warning to protect the roots by mulching in autumn.

Bergenias

Not everyone likes bergenias. Bergenias and gravel; bergenias and paving—we've heard it all before, ever since Gertrude Jekyll recommended them as edging plants. Nevertheless their handsome evergreen leaves do form invaluable bold contrasts to the mostly nondescript leaves of other herbaceous plants. And you do have to give *Bergenia crassifolia* (Zone 3) an extra mark for effort—it has been in cultivation since 1765, and you often see it peering from the debris of a derelict garden in spring, a quiet composition of light mauvy pink and green.

Among the white cultivars, 'Bressingham White' is excellent. The more I compare it to 'Silberlicht', the better it seems. 'Silberlicht' has

The leaves of Bergenia purpurascens *turn gleaming beetroot crimson for winter. This Himalayan elephant's ears makes a wonderful companion plant for pink and purple hellebores.*

OVERLEAF
For the richest purple flush to the leaves in winter, Bergenia *'Sunningdale' should be grown in sun. It was selected by Graham Stuart Thomas and introduced over thirty years ago.*

white flowers, becoming pinkish with age, cupped by attractive crimson sepals, but the ungainly leaves flop about, sometimes forming untidy umbrellas that hide the flowers. 'Bressingham White' is an altogether neater plant, slugs permitting.

Bergenias spread by their stout rhizomes which become elongated with time, but 'Silberlicht' seems more intent on climbing out of the ground, the result being woody-looking trunks with leaves of flabby leather at the ends. They must be divided and replanted firmly and more deeply, so the leaves of each section are just above soil level. *Bergenia stracheyi* 'Alba' (Zone 6) is a very nice diminutive thing, with pure white flowers that fade to shell pink. It looks good leaning on the stone in small paved areas.

The king of the bergenias must be the Irish cultivar 'Ballawley', raised in Dublin before 1950.

He is a magnificent fellow, all the larger if well fed, with splendid trusses of magenta flowers on tall, crimson-tinged stalks. The extra large, shining green leaves suffuse red at the first frost and, chameleonlike, turn green again overnight whenever the temperature goes up, even in winter. The more erect leaves of *Bergenia purpurascens*, on the other hand, turn gleaming beetroot red at the onset of cold weather and remain like that until spring, forming marvelous crimson pools of color. The contrast between the deep purple of the upper surface of the leaves and lighter red reverse makes each leaf seem backlit.

Bergenia ciliata (Zone 6) has yet another way of coping with cold: It simply acts as if it were deciduous, but some leaves persist through most Irish winters. The foliage is extraordinary to touch, being very hairy on both sides; the fleshy stalks are also hairy. The flowers are pale pink with reddish sepals.

A no-nonsense attitude is required toward bergenias. In spring, before they flower, I cut off any leaves that show the slightest blemish. If the clumps haven't been divided recently, a top dressing of fresh soil will conveniently disguise any exposed rhizomes, and encourages the plants to make further offsets.

Blue Foliage

Plants with wonderful blue-tinted foliage greatly appeal to me, none more so than *Berberis temolaica* (Zone 5). I wonder if this Tibetan shrub is scarce because it's hard to propagate. To me the leaves are ravishing, with a powdery bloom—glaucous, as a botanist would say—so they seem almost duck-egg blue. A nonscientific description of the flowers would be to say that they are like tiny upside-down lemon water lilies.

This lanky barberry grows to six feet or so, and doesn't object to a dryish position. You could say that it isn't a particularly shapely shrub, but this can always be adjusted by pruning out the weaker wood. There is a good, properly pruned specimen in the rose garden at Sissinghurst. As you can imagine, the gray-blue of the leaves charmingly complements the pinks, purples, and magentas of old-fashioned roses. The Chinese *Berberis dictophylla* (Zone 6) is similar, but the leaves not quite as large and its habit somewhat bushier.

Rudbeckia maxima (Zone 5) is a cause of intense irritation. I went to considerable trouble to acquire this coneflower, but only once has it produced a golden, drooping-petaled flower with prominent black central cone, despite its handsome, broad, blue-gray basal leaves. My plant has been in and out of a pot, moved up and down the garden, been given better soil, more moisture, and more sun *ad infinitum*. Shortage of sun in Ireland is, I think, a problem.

The honey flower, *Melianthus major* (Zone 8), from South Africa, has wondrous foliage of vivid blue-gray. In milder parts of Ireland it behaves true to its shrubby nature and produces spikes of browny-red flowers. But the older leaves seem lackluster compared to those of the current season, and I can do without the rather peculiar flowers. I like it best treated as an herbaceous plant, when by autumn it will have formed a mound of splendid, sculptured blue-green. It makes a good short-term container plant. *Melianthus minor* (Zone 9) was a small disappointment—less robust, the leaves nothing like so blue—and I decided it wasn't worth growing.

For years *Mertensia maritima* (Zone 3), the oyster plant, a rare Irish native, with fleshy powder-blue leaves and pink flowers turning to blue, happily seeded about. Then it just faded away. The longer you garden, the more often this sort of thing happens—who knows what nameless soil nutrient was suddenly depleted? However, *M. simplicissima* (Zone 6), true Asian form of *M. maritima*, which looks like a more vigorous version of the above, with irresistible glaucous leaves and clusters of pale blue flowers, is proving an excellent substitute. It is growing (as did *M. maritima*) in the equivalent, I hope, of a sandy beach—a gravelly mixture on a sunny raised bed. Both are adored by slugs and snails.

Caccinea strigosa (Zone 5) is a little-known member of the borage family with oval, bristly, pale blue leaves on sprawling stems and terminal panicles of blue flowers. Despite the delectable shade of the leaves, it is rather a coarse plant. Moreover, it cannot be disturbed, and must have sun and good drainage. It is best grown from seed. Chop its lax stems back to the base if it gets too untidy.

Cinquefoils

Nobody has ever written a eulogy about the European *Potentilla alba* (Zone 5), a thoroughly nice, plain sort of plant that will potter on in the same position forming a pleasant mound of gray-green palmate leaves with silvery-silky backs. About six inches tall, it is ideal for the front of the border, or for planting in paving or gravel. The flowers, like single white roses, have a wistful innocence and open for months on end. It prefers sun and is easily divided. I like *P. alba* so much, I have it growing in three different places,

Potentilla nitida (Zone 5) of the Alps is more demanding and requires a raised bed of gritty soil in full sun. The rare Irish form grown here, 'Lissadell', named after the nursery in County Sligo where it was selected, has deep rose-pink flowers, each petal veined with darker rose; this color intensifies at the base, making a delectable foil to the shining silvery carpet of neat little leaves. The whole plant is under three inches high. With a reputation of being shy of flowering, it never flowered better than last summer, the wettest of the century. Make a note to try giving it more water.

Potentilla fruticosa (Zone 2) and its innumerable cultivars, worthy plants as they are, are hard to get excited about. These shrubs look to me as if they are just about to be in full flower, or just over, but never in their prime; their lumpy shape adds little to the garden scene. They remind me

of an interminable meeting of shapeless men in gray suits where nothing is ever decided upon. The much-trumpeted launch of the red and pink cultivars on the gardening world was followed, here at any rate, by disappointment—the desire to acquire them was no sooner satisfied than I dug them up and threw them out. But on one occasion I did see the clear pink 'Princess' looking rather good, growing in part shade on rich Tipperary soil. And 'Vilmoriniana' is a desirable exception to the rule, redeemed by pretty silver leaves and soft yellow flowers.

'Monsieur Rouillard' (Zone 5) is an herbaceous plant. The sumptuous double flowers are composed of velvety, mahogany-red petals. The leaves are like those of a strawberry. The eighteen-inch stems flop about in a blowsy fashion on the edge of the red border, intermingling with those of one of its parents, the silver-leaved, red-flowered *P. atrosanguinea* (Zone 5).

Arguments rage about *P. nepalensis* 'Miss Willmott' (Zone 5). Does this illustrious lady have a right to be immortalized—yet again—by what is probably just a variant of the Himalayan species? Certainly, in this garden, the seedlings (of which there is always just the right number) never vary from their parent's typical cherry pink with black centers. She looks particularly fetching combined with black-green *Ophiopogon planiscapus* 'Nigrescens' (Zone 6).

Potentilla × *hopwoodiana* (Zone 5), an old (1829) hybrid between *P. nepalensis* and *P. recta*, is a recent arrival here. The unusual color of the flowers—a sort of creamy apricot with a strawberry center—is as pretty as it is difficult to place. Eventually I planted this charming antique with kniphofias, some of which are similar outcasts when it comes to color schemes.

Clematis

I used to worry very much about clematis wilt. If you don't know this distressing disease, it is the work of a fungus that attacks the plant, causing it to collapse suddenly. One day the plants are covered in lovely fat buds; the next day the stems and buds are pathetically limp, as if some nocturnal animal has bitten them off at ground level.

For several years, in an attempt to control wilt, the roots of all clematis here were drenched with fungicide every two weeks, but I couldn't say whether or not these efforts made much difference. But I do prepare a deluxe planting hole for each clematis, with at least four buckets of manure or garden compost per plant. This is not only to provide a rich root run but also to help retain moisture, for the worst cases of clematis wilt seem to happen in dry positions. A most cheering thought is that, in this garden at any rate, *C. viticella* (Zone 5) cultivars seem immune.

Cheating is always allowed in the garden. One effect to impress visitors has been made by planting two specimens of *C. viticella* 'Purpurea Plena Elegans' about six feet apart. Their flowers are

OVERLEAF
When it is right under my nose in the greenhouse, Clematis florida 'Sieboldii' gets properly looked after, and blossoms in early spring when little else is in flower.

deep murky purple, very double, reminding me of the hats that old ladies wear to church. The two plants are now a magic tangle of winding stems and murry purple blossom, intermingling with 'Mrs. Betty Corning' nearby. This latter is a heavenly clematis, the first American *C. viticella* cultivar, with beautiful pale blue, bell-shaped flowers, very flared at the rim. Viticellas normally bloom in late summer and autumn, but the first flowers on 'Mrs. Betty Corning' appear in June.

Of the reds, *C. viticella* 'Madame Julia Correvon', rich ruby red, also a little earlier than the others, is so good she is in three different places, while 'Venosa Violacea', violet with a paler center veined in purple, is in two. 'Alba Luxurians', a vigorous white cultivar with each sepal tipped in green, scrambles up a golden Irish yew (*Taxus baccata* 'Fastigiata Aurea'); 'Minuet', cream with a lavender picotee, is more delicate and is given a wrought iron arch on which to climb with no competition. *Clematis viticella*, the species itself, has smallish flowers but makes a generous display of little purple bells, each beautifully poised on a long, slender flower stalk, climbing through an old apple tree. As for 'Royal Velours', described invitingly as a "deep velvety purple," I am still housing several impostors and have yet to receive the true plant.

Perhaps gardeners would be less prone to anxiety if all clematis arrived with a note attached announcing their projected lifespan. *Clematis viticella* 'Etoile Violette' has been growing here for twelve years. Now long strips of bark are hanging off the thick woody stems at the base and the whole plant looks alarmingly vulnerable. I don't know if, in clematis terms, it's elderly or not—how much longer can it go on offering such a glorious mass of purple flower? Whereas I'd surmise that such strong species as *C. montana* (Zone 5) and *C. alpina* (Zone 4) are probably long lived, I secretly believe that the proper way to treat the large-flowered clematis is to love them, and if they wish to leave, too bad. Get another one.

But the large-flowered clematis are indeed wonderful plants, even if their built-in death wish necessitates a changeful collection. And if we stopped wanting to drape every patch of empty wall space with clematis, and planted them in more open positions instead, collections might remain more stable. 'Comtesse de Bouchaud' (not the prettiest pink in the world) has never suffered from wilt, but she's growing in a nice open position, likely to catch any summer rain going, as are 'Beauty of Worcester' (double deep blue, very nice), 'Marie Boisselot' (white, has never let me down), 'Duchess of Edinburgh' (superb double, masquerades as a frilly white rose), and 'Lasurstern' (large deep blue flowers, white anthers). There are no less than four different plants of 'Perle d'Azur' (divine, sky blue): growing through a silver pear tree, over a small myrtle, as a background to the mostly yellow back border, and on a wrought iron arch.

Clematis florida 'Sieboldii' (Zone 7), a lovely thing, looks more like a passionflower than a clematis, with creamy white flowers and a raised,

Clematis 'Duchess of Edinburgh' produces double flowers only on old wood, so don't be disappointed if you have single flowers for the first year after planting. Prune very sparingly.

deep violet, central boss. As it was said to be more tender than most, I tried it outside in a sheltered position. Such spots are invariably too dry, so I now grow it in the greenhouse where it can be watered regularly.

Clematis integrifolia (Zone 3) has dark blue-violet bell-shaped flowers on thirty-inch stems. If you've never seen an herbaceous, nonclimbing clematis before, this is an intriguing plant—not especially showy, but it makes a wonderful parent. Its union with *C.* ×*jackmanii* resulted in the inestimable *C.* ×*durandii* (Zone 5), a longtime success here in the blue border. Six-foot stems, draping themselves over and through nearby plants, present a long summer display of flowers in deepest violet-blue, and at the same time mask the remains of *Papaver orientale* 'Black and White' (Zone 3) after it has flowered. *Clematis integrifolia* crossed with *C. viticella* produced another excellent hybrid, *C.* ×*eriostemon*, a sprawling, semiwoody shrub that dearly needs another plant to grow through, in this case

Berberis dictophylla. The flowers are similar to those of *C. integrifolia.*

Clematis marmoraria (Zone 8) from New Zealand is very small indeed, under three inches in height, and rare in the wild. From a tuffet of glossy green, much-divided evergreen foliage arise single white flowers with a greenish tinge, aging to cream. It is a fussy little plant, too risky outdoors; once one has got over the initial thrill of owning such a curiosity, one's interest in it fades. But, when crossed with *C. paniculata* (Zone 5), a white-flowered climber to ten feet also from New Zealand, the result was *C. × cartmanii* 'Joe', a plant that far excels either parent.

'Joe' was named for its raiser, plantsman Joe Cartman. It is a nonclimbing shrub with shining, evergreen, dissected leaves and great panicles of white blossom in spring. The lax stems, to three feet or so, need training to a cane. 'Joe' blooms on the previous year's wood, so needs little pruning, except a tidy-up of weak stems after flowering. It is recommended as a plant for an alpine house, but I grow it in a large pot of peaty, gritty soil that is left outside the potting shed in the shade for most of the year and only comes under alpine house protection during the odd cold spell in winter. Note that the usual rule for clematis—a very rich potting mixture—is not recommended for the antipodeans. I gather that nitrogen is unacceptable to most New Zealand plants since there's so little in the natural soil there. Thus any New Zealand plants are potted in a mixture that is predominantly peat, sand, and grit.

I've mentioned grit several times already. What you use very much depends on what type of grit is available in your area—granite, flint, limestone, chippings, or whatever. Sometimes I use very small washed pebbles, like those of a gravel drive. For potting special items I usually wash the grit in several buckets of water to get rid of mud and very fine sand that might interfere with drainage.

Collector's Oddities

It is right that a collector's taste and interests should change as time progresses. Antique collectors start by being drawn toward the ornate decoration of the nineteenth century. Gradually they veer toward the restrained elegance of the eighteenth century, and finally the discriminating collector might enjoy only simple oak furniture with associated pewter, brass, and tin-glazed earthenware.

Such can be the progress of gardening taste. To begin with I thought dahlias were just the thing. Not for me the more delicate "cactus" or modest "pompon"; I wanted monster flowers as big as dinner plates. If they were bicolored, better still. Another plant that typifies this stage of my development was an annual, *Aster* 'Gusford Supreme', a startling bicolor in scarlet and white. Happily, this period didn't last too long, and the only survivor is the inestimable *Dahlia* 'Bishop of Llandaff'.

The next stage was a passion for the peculiar. The odder the plant, the more it appealed to me. The epitome of this branch line of gardening taste was *Rosa × odorata* 'Viridiflora'. Very novel. But soon its gloomy greeny-brown flowers (which are composed of clustered bracts rather than petals) began to pall, and the green rose went off to a plant sale.

The mandrake (*Mandragora officinarum*; Zone 6), a plant of sinister legend, is still in residence. I have never dared to examine the roots, for it was once believed that to dig up a mandrake is to die. These roots were thought to resemble a naked human and were believed to shriek if torn from the ground. (It was the shriek, apparently, that was fatal.) The suggested method of safe removal was to tie it to the tail of a sorcerer's dog. The transparent washy-blue flowers appear so early in spring that there are few pollinating insects around. But if you hand-pollinate them with a soft paintbrush, you get large bright green fruits that lie on the surface of the soil like unripe tomatoes, which is not surprising as both are members of the nightshade family, the Solanaceae. (In sunnier climates the fruits ripen to orange.) The standard gardening term, "resents disturbance," immediately brings to mind the mandrake—there aren't many plants that so resent being dug up that they would kill you for it.

The rose plantain, *Plantago major* 'Rosularis' (Zone 5), is a mutant I wouldn't be without. A tidy plant that doesn't overdo self-seeding, it has a flower spike in the form of a neat rosette of green petal-like leaves. *Plantago nivalis* (Zone 5), from the mountains of southern Spain, is also fun. This has neatly arranged silvery leaves and the appearance of a rare alpine, most deceiving until you notice the telltale plantain flowers. But my introduction to the garden of *Plantago major* 'Rubrifolia' was a mistake. Not only were the large maroon leaves permanently dusted with mildew, seedlings still turn up although the plant was officially removed years ago. *Plantago major* 'Variegata', nicely striped in cream and green, proved quite tricky to grow. To lose a plantain is embarrassing.

The hen-and-chickens daisy, *Bellis perennis* 'Prolifera' (Zone 3), in which the baby daisies cluster beneath the mother flower, is a delightful oddity, a variation on the common weed of lawns. The "chickens" appear as the main flower matures. It is easily lost unless it is divided annually and moved to a fresh spot.

Sometimes our wild plants produce monstrous forms, which gardeners perversely admire, although they would never dream of entertaining the original. This happens in every country, not just in Ireland. My own garden is home for the double form of our meadow buttercup, *Ranunculus acris* 'Flore Pleno' (Zone 5), with bright yellow button flowers. It needs good soil and frequent division to thrive. But beware the double creeping buttercup, *Ranunculus repens* 'Flore Pleno' (Zone 3). This has been in cultivation since the sixteenth century for the sake of its showy flowers packed with shining yellow petals. But here, even when planted in the gravel drive, its wandering ways became uncontrollable. *Ranunculus bulbosus* 'F. M. Burton', on the other hand, is a rather delicate plant with pretty lemon flowers. It causes anxiety by almost disappearing in summer, but then puts on fresh growth by autumn.

No sooner does a catalog say something like "the smallest in the world," than have it I must. *Viola verecunda* var. *yakusimana* (Zone 6) is a long name for a tiny viola. The whole plant is under half an inch tall. White flowers, delicately traced with purple, hover above the leaves. It sometimes gets killed in cold winters, but the odd seedling always turns up. Conversely, an enormous plant is equally tempting, such as *Megacarpaea polyandra* (Zone 7) from the Himalayas, a member of the Brassicaceae (formerly the Cruciferae). For eighteen years I waited for this plant to flower and produce its huge and remarkable seed pods, like those of a gigantic shepherd's purse or alyssum. But all that ever appeared were a few handsome, arching leaves. Finally I dug it up and threw it out. There are limits. According to a glowing testimonial on the genus, written in 1917, "At Kew and at Cambridge... where plants were grown for many years, *M. polyandra* never produced flowers." Most gratifying.

The sinister, brooding appearance of arisaemas (see also page 165) has special appeal for the collector. Himalayan *Arisaema griffithii* (Zone 8) is an evil-looking customer, more like a cobra steeling itself to strike than a flower. One large leaf is poised over the inflorescence like an individual umbrella. The stem is spotted and blotched with green and purple. The large flower (six inches at its widest) is murky purple and curiously netted. The tip of the spadix elongates into an astonishing two-foot tail-like extension. It blooms (if you can call it that) in April in a shady peat bed. Should there be a late frost, the flower and its umbrella turn into a sad mush. Arisaemas sometimes bide their time underground and don't show up for a year. They are not necessarily dead. The delicious contrast between strange plants, such as arisaemas, and obvious beauties of the plant world captures my imagination.

Corydalis

The flowers of *Corydalis flexuosa* are such a thrilling, vivid turquoise blue that they stop you in your tracks. Impossible to grow, you think. Like blue poppies and Asiatic gentians, plants of such ravishing coloring are bound to be difficult. But this corydalis is a surprisingly easy small plant (under one foot tall), given at least three requirements: light shade; leafy, gritty soil; and not too dry a position. It has racemes of slender, tubular flowers hovering over delicate, lacy-looking leaves. The blue of the flowers varies in intensity in the several different forms available, one of which has bronze leaves.

Corydalis flexuosa, introduced from China at the end of the 1980s, is rapidly filling the garden

Corydalis flexuosa, *introduced from China at the end of the 1980s, is surprisingly easy to grow in leafy, gritty soil. Propagate by division in early autumn.*

beds and is now leaping the garden walls, so easy is it to propagate; in early autumn, pull it into small pieces and replant them immediately. Nor does it mind being in a pot; indeed, potfuls of shimmering blue are yours for the asking. I keep mine in a shady place outside throughout the year, and divide the plants in early autumn to make further colonies.

Corydalis cashmeriana (Zone 5), with equally startling blue flowers, and *C. ambigua* of gardens

(syn. *C. fumariifolia*; Zone 6), paler but just as desirable, are from the Himalayas and Japan respectively. But these made feeble attempts to settle in Dublin and soon disappeared for good. Now, with the advent of *C. flexuosa*, I can marvel at this extraordinary shade of blue in several different parts of the garden. It is such a divine plant I don't care if it becomes so common that it suffers the ultimate indignity of being sold in supermarkets wrapped in cellophane.

It is recommendation indeed for a plant to be allowed space in my greenhouse for fourteen years, as has *Corydalis wilsonii* (Zone 7). I grow this as much for its duck-egg-blue foliage as for its bright yellow, green-tipped flowers on five-inch stems. It requires a largish pot and a very gritty mixture. At all times of year, go easy on the watering.

Now for a humble little weed, *Corydalis solida* (Zone 6). Like all good guests, arriving early and leaving early, the leaves appear in February and lilac-pink blossoms on six-inch stems follow in March. There's nothing left of it by May. There is no garden which hasn't the space for this—it will fit in anywhere, even among the crowns of later herbaceous plants. It increases rapidly, and autumn digging will expose a number of yellowish tubers. Pop them back and forget them. As yet the delectable, brick-red cultivar 'George P. Baker' is an uncommon, expensive treasure, an obvious candidate for a place of honor in a pot, although it multiplies much faster when planted out.

Corydalis lutea (Zone 6) is a wonderful, easy plant, around one foot tall, with bluish-green leaves like a maidenhair fern and bright yellow flowers that go on and on. But it becomes a major weed given half a chance, self-seeding in every direction, so I've moved it to shady gravel where it may colonize the whole area for all I care. *Corydalis ochroleuca* is similar, with creamy flowers, but is better behaved and provides just the right amount of offspring—two seedlings for me and three to give away.

Daisies

People are affected by daisies in different ways: They either love the simple shape of the flower, because it reminds them of daisies they saw on the lawn as a child, or hate them and stroll on by saying, "Yet another boring composite." There are about 21,000 species in the Asteraceae (formerly the Compositae), the enormous daisy family, some of which I'm especially keen on.

You'd guess *Aster thomsonii* (Zone 6) from the Himalayas would be a good plant, as it is one of the parents of *A.* ×*frikartii*, which gave us that famous, long-flowering paragon of a cultivar, 'Mönch'. The small form, *A. thomsonii* 'Nanus', is about two feet tall (or a bit more if well fed) and produces month after month a succession of clear lavender-blue daisies. (In photographs the flowers always have a pink tinge.) This plant makes all notions of restraint go out the window—it's such good value, I'd like 'Nanus' in every bed in the garden. In my experience this aster resents being divided, even in the recommended season of spring. It also needs fertile soil and sun.

Anthemis punctata subsp. *cupaniana* (Zone 5) is the first plant I'd suggest for edging a new bed. Its fluffy mounds of aromatic silver-gray foliage would take away the empty look and rapidly soften the edges. Crisp white daisies appear for months. As soon as the plant begins to sprawl, cut it back hard, and it'll soon start all over again. Ideal for dry places, it requires sun and good drainage.

An all-time beauty among foliage plants, Senecio candidans *from Patagonia and the Falkland Islands thrives only in a cool position with constant slug control.*

It never ceases to surprise me that the horrid weed, common groundsel (*Senecio vulgaris*), should have beautiful relations. One such, which came to me labeled as *Senecio populifolius*, turns out to be a probably unnamed pericallis from the Canary Islands. The leaves, reminiscent of a white poplar, well justify its former name; they are glossy gray-green above, white-woolly beneath. The stems are also covered in silvery white hairs. Corymbs of daisylike flowers, appearing nonstop from April to autumn, are white with magenta centers, washed with magenta at the tips of the rays, in effect like a most refined florist's cineraria (*Pericallis* × *hybrida*). But whereas the showy flowers of the latter are offset by coarse green

leaves, the flowers of my anonymous pericallis are displayed to full advantage by the silvery foliage. A fleeting scent of vanilla can be detected, more pronounced on sunny days. Planted in the greenhouse border, trained to wires on the wall, mine is now around five feet tall. It is easy from cuttings, and makes a good container plant, but the only place I've seen it thus used is at Sissinghurst in Kent. This excellent plant has survived the annual purge in a seriously overcrowded greenhouse for the past twelve years.

Senecio candidans (Zone 7) comes from the remote beaches and sand dunes of southern Patagonia and the Falkland Islands. In the wild its leaves huddle close to the ground as defense

Celmisia semicordata *'David Shackleton' (with green* Zigadenus elegans*) flourishes on the raised bed in the Sundial Garden within easy reach of the water barrel. Celmisias, also known as New Zealand daisies, hate dry conditions during the growing season.*

against the ceaseless wind, but in cultivation they become glistening ovals of silver. A temperate climate, a cool position, and remorseless destruction of nearby slugs are required for its successful cultivation. Thick roots, creeping about on the surface of the soil, allow Irishman's cuttings as a method of propagation. Any illusions about this, an all-time beauty among foliage plants, are shattered by the grubby little yellow flowers, which unfortunately reveal its groundselly nature.

On the other hand, *Senecio pulcher* (Zone 8), also from South America, has stunning, large, brilliant magenta daisies with yellow centers clustered atop stout stems in autumn. The dark green, leathery, eight-inch-long, lightly toothed leaves are attractive to slugs. This unusual plant needs a position that is often tricky to find, one that affords shelter, fertile soil, plenty of sun, is dryish in winter and nicely moist in summer—perhaps at the base of a wall. Propagate it by careful division in spring.

Many gardeners, thrilled by possession of a coveted celmisia, one of the silver-leaved New Zealand daisies, plant it in a cozy corner, protected by a shrub, and proceed to worry about winter wet. They won't need to worry for long, for the celmisia will shortly disappear.

How many times, when reading about silver-leaved plants, have we been told, "Dry position required." But celmisias are a notable exception to this blanket rule: Some of them grow in areas with 300 inches of rain per year. But on no account do they want a bog; in fact, they need

good drainage, but they do need masses of water. Another example of gardening lore on the cultivation of gray-leaved plants refers to the necessity of a warm, sheltered site. This may be due to the fact that many such plants are of Mediterranean origin. But celmisias in the wild are often found at considerable altitude, on cold, windswept mountain slopes and fell fields, or growing among tussock grasses, fully exposed to strong sun. The "silver" in these plants is a coating of hairs that do two things: reflect back harmful ultraviolet light and protect the leaves from the desiccating effect of wind.

So before you fall for the idea of growing New Zealand daisies, note their requirements: a peaty, gritty soil low in nitrogen; cool summers; mild winters; high rainfall; copious summer watering in drought; and an entirely open position exposed to wind and sun. Acid soil is usually recommended, but I don't think this is essential, provided all the other requirements are met. Propagation is by very fresh seed or by early autumn division. You will find when dividing celmisias that most sections come away without root—simply insert the pieces very firmly up to the base of the leaf rosette and roots will form during winter.

New Zealand daisies are not only collectors' plants but also spectacular in the garden. *Celmisia semicordata* (Zone 7), probably the most handsome and easy for garden display, has foot-high rosettes of lustrous silver—evergreen, spiky, and wonderful in winter. Large, pure white daisies with yellow centers on silvery white stems appear in early summer. To keep the plants looking smart, any dead leaves can be pulled off with a sharp downward tug in autumn.

Celmisia semicordata 'David Shackleton' has dazzling spiky platinum leaves. (The flowers are usually somewhat deformed, but no matter—they're easily cut off.) Not as easy as the species itself, which can almost be treated as a bedding plant, this cultivar grows in a peaty raised bed in close proximity to the water barrel.

With none of the dash and swagger of the foregoing are two humble little daisies, *Erigeron philadelphicus* (Zone 2), a foot-high native of the northern United States and Canada with little mauve-pink flowers, and *Bellis rotundifolia* 'Caerulescens' (Zone 8), with pretty, pale blue flowers on four-inch stems. You wouldn't notice either in a crowd, but both are charming small plants, useful for filling in. Both self-seed mildly.

Daphnes

In spite of their unpredictable behavior, I have a sort of reverence for daphnes. To collect them is a continuous pattern of delight followed by despair, with some variation in the length of time between the two, for they are as capable of sudden collapse as they are of lingering death.

After ten years, my third *Daphne cneorum* (Zone 5), the divinely scented rose-pink garland flower, has had to be taken out. Several years ago, the leaves of one twig turned yellow. Thinking nothing of it, I cut it off. The following year, a larger branch displayed similar symptoms. This too was cut off. The decay continued, as I told myself lies about inadvertent feet, stray dogs, and so on. Anyone who has grown a daphne, with the exception of the stalwart, shade-tolerant, decent and boring *Daphne laureola* (Zone 7), needn't be told the rest of the story.

But *Daphne cneorum*, recalcitrant as she may be, is one of the parents of a defiantly easy and excellent plant, *Daphne × burkwoodii* 'Somerset' (Zone 5). The proverbial "hybrid vigor" so often spoken of by plantspeople certainly applies to 'Somerset', with its abundant clusters of fragrant, blush-pink flowers, borne on healthy, four-foot-high, semi-evergreen bushes.

Daphne petraea 'Grandiflora' (Zone 6), number four, looks reasonably good in its clay pot in the alpine frame, with plenty of fat flower buds. Apparently this delicious little daphne, the cause of Reginald Farrer's more extravagant prose, flowers better when underpotted; you just hope that the flowering stage takes place before the dying stage. I never let the pot dry out. In the same class but less pernickety is *Daphne arbuscula* (Zone 6), a delectable, neat little shrub about a foot high, with intensely fragrant rosy flowers. For years I had a good specimen in full sun and limy soil. Half-ripe cuttings of young shoots will root in midsummer or just after.

I have given up growing the much-loved, winter-blooming mezereon, *Daphne mezereum* (Zone 4), with scented flowers in lilac-pink to violet-red, or sometimes white. *The New Royal Horticultural Society Dictionary of Gardening* tells me that this is a short-lived plant. Quite. It is also prone to viral disease—if you examine plants for sale you'll notice some already infected. I suspect *Daphne odora* 'Aureomarginata' (Zone 8) is riddled with the same thing. I have twice possessed *Daphne genkwa* (Zone 5), the one with flowers of melted amethyst, but it so resents the chains of cultivation (at least here in Dublin) that I haven't the heart to try again.

But *Daphne bholua* (Zone 8) is going from strength to strength, with no sign of the V word. The dullish, leathery evergreen leaves and clusters of rosy-mauve flowers are not especially showy. But so sublime is its winter scent that it makes you think of giddy, summer days; delicious wafts are dispensed for yards around to be sniffed half a garden away. Flowers appear for two months at least, but the first flush is the greatest, opening on warm winter days, often just after Christmas. If I lived in too cold an area to grow this outside, it would be one of the first plants granted space in a cool conservatory. It sends up occasional suckers from the base to pot up as extras. Protected from cold winds in a sheltered sunny corner, this Himalayan shrub is now eight feet tall, while a deciduous form, *Daphne bholua* 'Gurkha', which originated at a higher altitude and is therefore considered hardier, thrives in an open position.

Enjoyable arguments about whether one of my daphnes was *D. retusa* or *D. tangutica* have been spoiled; it is now correctly *D. tangutica* Retusa Group (Zone 6). One of the neatest small shrubs, this is far less particular than most species. It makes a nicely rounded, evergreen mound profusely decorated with highly fragrant clusters of flowers, rose-purple on the outside, white suffused purple inside. It likes a lot of humus. I suspect one of the reasons I find daphnes not all that easy is that they dislike dry soil. *Daphne retusa* does well for about

*Angel's fishing rod, or wand flower (*Dierama pulcherrimum*), looks best when planted in an isolated position to display its graceful habit.*

ten years (I am now on my third). After thoughtful provision of a few self-sown seedlings, it then starts to look moth-eaten and is best replaced.

Dieramas

You cannot imagine a more graceful plant than the angel's fishing rod or wand flower, *Dierama pulcherrimum* (Zone 8), a South African member of the iris family. The stems form great sweeping arches of bell-like flowers that tremble in the slightest breeze. Suspended by nigh invisible pedicels, the flowers open from silvery, papery calyxes, in a succession that starts from the tip of the stem. They may be pale pink, rose-pink, deep mauve-pink, purple, or white.

Various small dieramas can be seen in Irish gardens, in particular a little one with satiny, coral-pink flowers opening from pale brown, papery bracts on fifteen-inch stems, with quickly spreading grassy foliage. Could this be *D. dracomontanum*? Confusion reigns. This species is said to be very variable in flower color, but my plant's seedlings are perfect replicas of the parent, so I suspect it is indeed a species.

The Slieve Donard nursery in Northern Ireland, now sadly no longer in existence, made a specialty of the genus in the fifties and selected many seedlings, some named after Shakespearian characters—'Oberon', 'Puck', and so on—and some after birds—'Blackbird', for example, is said to be a most desirable dark purple cultivar. Three different so-called 'Blackbird's are here, but I'm not sure I have confidence in any of their credentials. The search for these original cultivars, by all those interested in dieramas, has been like a quest for the Holy Grail. But it has perhaps been unnecessary, for, in my experience, dieramas produce seedlings either very similar to the parents, or, if a little different, every bit as good. Two medium-size dieramas in this garden, in white and palest pink, are particular favorites—they are almost certainly descendants of the Slieve Donard originals.

To show off their pendulous stems, dieramas should be given an isolated position—on a corner, a path edge, or in gravel. They need full sun and (the usual contradiction in terms) moist but well-drained soil. Their evergreen leaves need a good tidy-up in spring. Don't lose patience and yank the dead leaves away in a hurry, or you will pull away the fibrous tunics of the corms below the soil level, to the detriment of the plant.

Like young grass, self-sown seedlings come up all around the plants. Would that there were space to grow them all on for comparison. As regards division, we are advised that dieramas dislike being disturbed, but there comes a stage when an old plant has become such a congested mass that action must be taken. Furthermore, with something special such as the white one, the seedlings might be white, but to be absolutely sure, division is necessary.

Dividing a dierama is a fraught operation. Dig up the parent plant with great care. Extending beneath the corms you will find fat, white, fleshy, easily broken roots, as well as stringy older ones. The aim is to avoid damaging these appendages. My plants are divided in autumn, potted individually, and kept under glass for the winter.

Doubletalk

Of the numerous double daffodils, none catches my imagination more than Queen Anne's double daffodil, named not in honor of the English Queen Anne, but for Anne, Princess of Austria in the seventeenth century. (There's disagreement about whether she became queen of France or of Spain.) An exquisite, rare old daffodil, the pale yellow flowers nod toward the soil, as if weighed down by all its years in cultivation. It is now correctly known by the less romantic name of *Narcissus* 'Eystettensis'. In spite of having a Latin name as if it were a species, this plant has never been found in the wild. It has been suggested that it is a mutation of some small primrose-colored trumpet daffodil. But there is no doubt that Queen Anne's double daffodil has been cherished by gardeners for hundreds of years.

I make a special fuss over this plant. It is growing in two different parts of the garden, a precaution I use for most rare items. A close eye is kept on its health—if a patch doesn't look as good as the previous year, I divide the bulbs, discarding any that seem unhealthy. I always divide daffodils immediately after flowering, when I'm thinking about them, and can concentrate on where they'd look well the following spring. Have you noticed that however carefully their positions are marked, if you try hunting for daffodil bulbs in August, invariably some get sliced in half with the spade? Another reason for spring division is that I can see where the dying leaves are not going to be too obvious. Because the tired soil of a garden started in 1830 might not be to their liking, the planting area is prepared with fresh topsoil and bonemeal. I then make an individual hole for each bulb, pop it in, and flood the hole with water before filling in with soil. The charming old bright yellow double 'Rip van Winkle' needs watching likewise.

As you've probably discovered, lily of the valley has a mind of its own. If it is put in too good a position, it romps everywhere. Sometimes, exiled to a dry spot, it doesn't budge. The double lily of the valley, *Convallaria majalis* 'Prolificans' (Zone 3), has been too slow to increase at the foot of an apple tree and must be moved to a better position. But nearby the double Solomon's seal, *Polygonatum odoratum* 'Flore Pleno' (Zone 4), is spreading nicely, encouraged by generous helpings of compost. The fragrant little cream bells, with extra petals inside, washed with green at the tips, warrant close examination.

An exceptionally fine double buttercup, *Ranunculus constantinopolitanus* 'Plenus' (Zone 6), flowers in May, producing large rosettes of glossy yellow petals, brilliant green in the middle. Buttercups in general, in fact most members of the Ranunculaceae, enjoy rich living in moist soil. I keep an emergency plant of this growing in a different spot.

The double *Delphinium* 'Alice Artindale' (Zone 4) is so prone to mildew, one wonders if Alice herself suffered from consumption. But it is a rather special plant, with five-foot spires of very double flowers, mostly turquoise blue with a dash of green and mauve. 'Alice Artindale' will bloom again in September, as long as she is cut to the ground immediately after the first flush, given copious cans of water, lavish handfuls of fertilizer, and a mulch of two buckets of either manure or compost.

Spiderworts are like nice but unexciting people—I find they're hard to become enthusiastic about. But *Tradescantia virginiana* 'Caerulea Plena' (Zone 5) is a pleasant plant, with double, mid-blue flowers, useful for unimportant places where its typically messy foliage won't draw attention.

Old gardening books torment us with descriptions of the double sweet rocket, *Hesperis matronalis* 'Alba Plena' (Zone 3). The first plants of these (given to me by Molly Sanderson, the celebrated Northern Irish gardener for whom the coke-black, yellow-eyed *Viola* 'Molly Sanderson' was named) were too weak from virus to make much effort to grow. Fortunately, virus-free stock of this elusive old plant is now available. So many scented double white flowers on tall spikes, rather like those of stock, appear in early summer that rich soil is essential to support the show. The effort of flowering can be too much, so 'Alba Plena' is best treated as a biennial and propagated every year from basal cuttings, or better still, from an Irishman's cutting.

There are double bellflowers aplenty: from pretty little fairies' thimbles (*Campanula cochleariifolia*; Zone 6), and *C.* × *haylodgensis* 'Plena' (Zone 5), only a few inches high, to several different forms of the peach-leaved bellflower (*C. persicifolia*; Zone 3), in both blue and white, some of which are more double than others. The one for connoisseurs is *C. trachelium* 'Albo Plena' (Zone 3). Not a very vigorous plant, this double white form of the nettle-leaved bellflower is best propagated by careful division in late summer. All the double bellflowers are beautiful.

Fussy Antique Plants

It is said that the rose 'La France' was the first hybrid tea. Dating from 1865, it has silvery pink flowers and a sweet, old-fashioned scent. It also has a weak constitution, as befits a grande dame of the rose world, and suffers from black spot, mildew, and rust, usually all at once. Aphids, always attracted by an ailing plant, find 'La France' irresistible. For years I fussed with it,

ever ready with the sprayer, but eventually gave up the struggle; nice as it is to own a delicate antique, one can tire of being a constant nursemaid.

But fair maids of France, *Ranunculus aconitifolius* 'Flore Pleno' (Zone 6), is quite another matter. Also called white bachelor's buttons or fair maids of Kent, it is said to have Huguenot connections and was known in cultivation in England by 1597. I suspect the reason that it is rare owes much to its being weakened by vegetative propagation over the years. But for the sake of its adorable, neat buttons of pure white, it warrants any amount of attention. To compensate for its lack of stamina, I give it the richest possible soil. For years it prospered on the same site, and then began to dwindle. Rescued, moved to a new site with fresh soil, it is once more gathering strength. (Rotation cropping may be as desirable for flowers as it is for vegetables.) With a rare plant such as this, I try to keep an emergency plant in a different part of the garden. Apart from anything nasty underground, this is also a good precaution against an enemy of the two-legged kind.

Auriculas were mentioned by John Gerard in his wonderful *Herbal* of 1597, and are said to have been introduced to England in the sixteenth century by Huguenot silk weavers. Auriculas became very popular in eighteenth-century Dublin, where they were grown and exhibited by the aristocracy and were later adopted by the artisans of northern England. You can imagine how these flowers illuminated their monotonous, working lives—the velvety texture of the petals,

Auriculas and Primula marginata cultivars—magical plants worth any amount of trouble—are protected by glass to stop winter rains from washing away the lovely powder on their leaves.

Auriculas were popular in eighteenth-century Dublin, where they were grown and exhibited by the aristocracy. A neat white circle in the center of the flower signified a good specimen.

vibrant colors, and immaculate circles of white farina all add to their jewel-like quality.

For years I grew auriculas badly. I kept them outside all year, where they suffered too much from wet Irish winters. 'Old Double Green' and 'Old Irish Blue', both scarce plants, were probably already infected with virus when they arrived. At that stage I didn't know what a virus was, but I did think that the yellow spotting on the leaves was suspicious. Whenever you collect a lot of plants in the same genus, you run the risk of getting a dis-ease that could wipe out the lot. So I threw away my entire auricula collection and started again.

Auriculas are believed to be hybrids of mysterious origin, probably descendants of two mountain primroses, *Primula auricula* and *P. rubra*. The last thing they need is to be coddled, so I ordered a special frame with copious ventilation. Their potting mixture is based on roughly one-third each of fresh soil, grit, and leaf mold. Crumbled old manure, well-rotted garden compost, and bonemeal are also added for their delectation.

What exactly do I mean by this? Each year I make a note of the precise proportions used, thinking that if they do well in that mixture, I'll be able to use the same again. But the following year, I make up a different compost in an effort to find the optimum concoction.

Ideally, auriculas should be repotted immediately after flowering, in early May, to give the young roots all summer to develop. The potted auriculas stay outside all summer in the shade and are watered regularly, occasionally with liquid fertilizer. They seem to have a spurt of growth in early autumn and are then tidied up by pulling off the old leaves with a little tug. (This should be done in a downward direction or the whole plant may snap off.) Lurking slugs are picked off, and any algae or moss is cleaned from the pots. They are then moved to their frame, which is placed to catch the winter sun. For the next few months they need very little water. When I asked an expert grower from Northern Ireland exactly how much he watered his plants, he answered, "Up here I keep them as dry as a cactus." Still, they need to be checked regularly. Another cleanup of old leaves will be necessary after Christmas. Toward flowering time they will require much more water, and liquid feed once a week.

Primula marginata cultivars such as 'Marven' (mauve-blue with a white farinose eye), 'White Linda Pope' (greenish white, very fetching), and 'Elizabeth Fry' (pale lavender) are not auriculas but are treated exactly the same way. To make a real show of these, I plant several different plants two to three inches apart in a seven-inch pot. This is quite a complicated procedure, liable to bring on bad temper and best accomplished out of earshot of anyone else. Try keeping the compost fairly loose while you juggle the plants about, and don't firm them in until all are neatly arranged.

Sometimes antique plants have odd connotations, for example *Dianthus* 'Mrs. Sinkins'. Mrs. Sinkins was the matron of Slough Poor Law Institution in southern England during the late nineteenth century. Her namesake is scented. Although hauntingly delicious, this perfume still brings cold corridors and watery soup to mind. And how about the annual *Limnanthes douglasii*, the poached-egg flower from California? I can only ever think of poor David Douglas, its discoverer, and his untimely death in a pit dug to trap wild animals. This cheerful little plant has perpetuated his memory in my garden for the last twenty years, with a self-seeding patch of yellow flowers with white-tipped petals. But, far from thinking of poached eggs, I'm too busy wondering exactly which animal it was in the pit.

The Garden Walls

Selecting what to grow beside the garden walls provokes the usual dilemma: The designer in me insists on clothing the walls in plain green leaves, using quiet background sub-

Allium aflatunense (bottom left), geraniums, and erodiums beside the path leading to the Iris Garden. Red Salvia microphylla var. neurepia is tucked into a sheltered corner to the left of the wrought iron arch.

jects, such as ivy, yew, pyracantha, and pittosporum, while the plantsman bit of me totally disagrees, and wants to reserve the space for special, often tender items. The plants mentioned below, valued old friends, are those on whose presence a unanimous decision has been reached.

Itea ilicifolia (Zone 7) was discovered and introduced by the renowned Irish plant collector Augustine Henry (1857–1930), who found it growing near the Yangtze Gorge in China. Long before my time, Dr. Henry lived next door, at 47 Sandford Road. Some of the plants he introduced, such as the glorious light orange August-flowering *Lilium henryi*, do unusually well here—in my more fanciful moments I imagine his benevolent ghost smiling over the wall. Henry's itea has evergreen, hollylike leaves, shiny dark green above, paler beneath; it makes a great bulging shrub on the north wall of the house. The fragrant racemes of pale green tiny flowers, reminiscent of love-lies-bleeding or tassel flower, appear in August, just when cool green is most desired.

A flowering gooseberry cunningly disguised as a fuchsia, *Ribes speciosum* (Zone 7), from California, is now ten feet tall on the west wall. The fresh young leaves, a reviving sight in early February, are glossy dark green. The young shoots are reddish and the whole plant is razor prickly. In spring the bush is alive with little tubular crimson flowers with long stamens. Alas, there are no hummingbirds in Dublin to pollinate the flowers, so no gooseberries. I prune it lightly each summer to keep it within bounds.

Cestrum parqui (Zone 9) from Chile has always behaved as a shrub on the east wall, but I've seen it in colder gardens used as an herbaceous plant, cut annually to the ground by frost. The linear, mid-green leaves are uninspiring and foetid, particularly when cut by secateurs. But the dense panicles of tiny, starry flowers in late summer are a refined, soft greenish yellow. The flowers have an unpleasant odor that changes at dusk to a heavy sweet scent, seductive to moths I presume.

The white form of the potato vine, *Solanum jasminoïdes* 'Album' (Zone 9), will delicately entwine itself through nearby shrubs. Clusters of pure white flowers appear in profusion from late summer on. If it is not killed back in winter, it can reach twenty feet, but is probably all the better for hard spring pruning to five feet or so. On the sunny east wall it rambles through cherry-red *Salvia microphylla* var. *neurepia* (Zone 9). This excellent salvia is now seven feet tall in a sheltered corner, a mass of flowers and aromatic foliage for many months in summer. Incidentally, every gardening book I've looked at to date recommends *S. jasminoïdes* 'Album', undeniably beautiful as it is, in preference to the species itself, which is described as a "washy blue"; such comments notwithstanding, I find its watery blue flowers unusually pretty.

To brush past *Acacia pravissima* (Zone 8) in April invites showers of golden dust from its bright yellow bobbly flowers, scented on warm days. Considered one of the hardiest Australian wattles, it grows in the narrow east-facing bed near the greenhouse. The arching stems of almost fernlike blue-green foliage (apparently phyllodes rather than leaves) hang down gracefully, making this a beautiful small tree at all times. *A. pravissima* is fast growing and doesn't care for being cut back into old wood, although a light pruning is acceptable immediately after flowering.

The wattle is trying to oust the Mexican *Beschorneria yuccoïdes* (Zone 9) at its feet, one of the most exotic-looking plants grown in Ireland. In spring, if flowering is imminent, this beschorneria presents a bud huge with promise, from which a very robust, deep salmon-pink stem gradually extends to about eight feet in length, at which point a carillon of emerald bells erupts from rosy bracts. The gray-green, lance-shaped leaves form a basal rosette up to five feet tall. Although it is growing in a sheltered place, I usually construct a protective plastic film tent over the plant in winter. Don't deadhead it; the pink flowering stems remain decorative through summer.

Buddleja crispa (Zone 8) from the Himalayas, growing at the foot of the south wall near the greenhouse, has prettier foliage than most butterfly bushes—the leaves are a downy, silvery gray-green. Even the flower stalks are soft and woolly-looking. A long succession of sweetly fragrant clusters of lilac-colored flowers appears from midsummer into autumn. *Clematis* 'Venosa Violacea' (Zone 6) wanders through it. *Buddleja crispa* will not tolerate hard pruning into old wood, as you would do with *B. davidii*.

Over the years many different contenders on the borderline of hardiness have hustled for space in the sheltered spot beneath the buddleja. Notable failures include *Eryngium proteiflorum* (Zone 8), which only thought about flowering once in the middle of winter; *Cyclamen graecum* (Zone 9), which produced only a few hesitant leaves; and *Ixia viridiflora* (Zone 9), which had to be moved to greater protection near the alpine house. But *Puya alpestris* (Zone 8), a bromeliad from Chile, has made several rosettes of shiny, gray-green, silver-backed leaves, barbed like fish hooks. And *Nerine bowdenii* 'Alba' (listed as Zone 9, but I'd say it's hardier) is increasing happily, and presents an autumn parade of white flowers faintly blushed with pink. Needless to say, this warm, dry spot is much relished by the deep violet-blue *Iris unguicularis* 'Mary Barnard' (Zone 7).

The tea rose 'Général Schablikine' (1878) doesn't appear to be common, but its virtues were sung in 1898 by Lord Brougham (the carriage was named after his uncle) in his book about the roses at Château Eléonore, in Cannes: "If a law was passed that one man should cultivate but one variety of rose I should without hesitation choose 'Général Schablikine'… This of all roses serves us the most faithfully and generously." Quite so. Trained on the east wall, it is never without flower except just after pruning. The fragrant, soft coppery pink flowers are very double, flat, and old-fashioned looking.

Also on the east wall is *Azara microphylla* 'Variegata' (Zone 8), a small evergreen tree from

Chile and Argentina. Sprays of little shiny leaves, variegated in cream, give the tree a light and frothy effect. Numerous tiny yellow flowers, highly fragrant of vanilla, appear in February, the scent wafting for yards around. The tree casts little shade, thus allowing a patch of *Cyclamen libanoticum* (Zone 9) to flourish underneath, tucked in a dry place beside the wall. This has light rose-pink petals with a small crimson-magenta blotch at the base and marbled gray-green leaves. This lovely winter-flowering cyclamen used to be in a pot in the alpine house, but it seems far happier outside. The flowers have a nose-tickling, musty odor.

Tree peonies, heavenly as they are, make me think of burst water pipes. Gardening books have it that the young growth of tree peonies mustn't be exposed to the early morning sun—I assume the melting ice expands inside the shoots, the way frost damages water pipes.

One divine tree peony, *Paeonia suffruticosa* (Zone 5), grows near the walls of the alpine house, in the worst possible east-facing position. With total disregard for late frosts, this foolish plant rashly unfolds new leaves and prominent flower buds, in mid-February if you please. By the time I'd discovered about the correct placement for tree peonies it was too late, and they're not the sort of plants to be shuffled around at whim. For years I used to go out early on frosty mornings and throw a rug over it.

I believe my plant is descended from one of the first early imports to arrive in the West, now seen rarely in old Irish gardens. This peony is depicted on *famille rose* eighteenth-century Chinese porcelain that has the large pink flower in the center of the design. And it could well be the very same double pink tree peony of which Maria Edgeworth, the Irish author (1768–1849), said: "My peony tree is the most beautiful thing on earth—19 flowers will be in full blow next week. Poor dear Lord Oriel gave it me and his own is dead and he is dead. But love for him still lives in me." (Lord Oriel had given her the mudan that was imported from China for the Royal Gardens at Kew by Sir Joseph Banks in 1789).

I'm uncertain about the grafted tree peonies imported from Japan: you often can't see their flowers because they're hidden by the leaves, and I've yet to see a really thriving specimen. However, the Dr. Saunders hybrids raised in the United States are superb—compact and floriferous, with flowers that you can see. 'High Noon', with sumptuous double flowers in ripe lemon yellow, grows in the shade of the north wall.

Nearby is the most wanton, extravagant beauty of the garden, *Paeonia suffruticosa* 'Joseph Rock' (also known as subspecies *rockii* or 'Rock's Variety'). Still very rare in Europe, this is available in the United States, whence mine came. The single flowers are enormous. Frilled creamy-white petals, satiny to the touch and splodged with liquid crimson-purple at the base, surround a boss of quivering golden stamens.

OVERLEAF

The tree peony beside the Alpine House in April. Tree peonies are not the sort of plant to be shuffled around at whim, so I daren't move it, although it's in the worst possible east-facing position.

Brunnera macrophylla 'Langtrees' has wonderfully spotted leaves and isn't fussy about soil or position. This clump has been in the same place under the 'Bramley' apple for fifteen years.

Good Plants for Bad Places

The garden is a most undemocratic place. Consider the aristocrats of the plant world. These demand good drainage, insist on either sun or shade, refuse to grow unless on lime-free soil, require winter protection, threaten to die unless constantly propagated, and issue an ultimatum that they will fade away forthwith unless moved to the best position in the garden.

But at the bottom of the scale is the honest, workhorse type of plant, the sort you leave in the same place for ten years or more. *Brunnera macrophylla* (Zone 3) is one such paragon. In an ideal world, no doubt brunnera would prefer moist, humus-rich conditions. But even in some forgotten corner in dryish shade, it still produces delicate sprays of blue forget-me-nots and conveniently smothers any adventurous weeds with large, heart-shaped leaves. The cultivar 'Langtrees' has leaves decorated with large silvery spots and is equally resistant to neglect. 'Hadspen Cream' produces pale green leaves variegated in cream and is given slightly better treatment, still in shade but with more moisture at the root. 'Dawson's White' is in quite another category; its leaves are prettily variegated in dark green and white, but the white portions are easily scorched when exposed to cold wind and too much sun— a plant for what, in real estate agent's terms, would be called "first-class accommodation."

The mourning widow, *Geranium phaeum* (Zone 5), may not be the showiest geranium around, but the reflexed little gloomy maroon flowers deserve close inspection. The widow will grow and flower just about anywhere, but I like best the white form, 'Album', which has rather larger flowers. 'Variegatum' is a little disappointing, with indiscriminate blotchy variegation, but is pleasing in autumn, once the older leaves have been cut away. *Geranium phaeum* spreads by seed, and is exactly the sort of plant I want for an unsalubrious spot.

The dependable, classic plant for tolerating neglect is *Geranium macrorrhizum* (Zone 4). The purplish-pink flowers are not exciting, but the plant is redeemed by excellent, weed-smothering, strongly aromatic foliage. Its clone 'Variegatum' looks best in spring, when the young leaves show smart variegation.

Geranium procurrens (Zone 6) is charm itself in early autumn, when its purple-pink flowers with black centers frolic over every other plant within range. Meanwhile, beneath the mass of foliage, it is quietly annexing territory, busily forming new plantlets at each leaf joint. The very devil in your best bed, if grown in the garden equivalent of a slum *G. procurrens* is an excellent plant, provided you remain in total charge, ruthlessly removing surplus plantlets in spring. *Geranium endressii* is just as accommodating and not invasive. It sprawls around producing a generous, endless supply of bright pink flowers. Just give it a short back and sides occasionally and fresh foliage and flowers will soon appear. This geranium still thrives in the same spot in my garden, having been divided only once in fifteen years.

Certain plants can prove too much of a good thing. The variegated ground elder, *Aegopodium podagraria* 'Variegatum' (Zone 2), and the white form of the rosebay willowherb, *Epilobium angustifolium* 'Album' (Zone 3), are two superlative examples. Both had perfect manners when first planted, the ground elder producing a modest quantity of pale green leaves splashed with cream, and the willowherb a few beguiling spires of white. By the time I had decided they had got out of hand, it was too late. So, unless these two beautiful, far too rapacious weeds can be corralled, beware. I have seen the ground elder used brilliantly in a Canadian garden, forming a shining, wide ribbon of pale, creamy green foliage, brightening the shade between scrubby woodland and lawn. In another place the plant was imprisoned between a stream and a gravel path; all attempts it made to move from these two chosen spots were cut short by vigorous mowing.

When it comes to these easy species, I keep asking myself, Does this particular plant need such a good spot? If it would do just as well under

a hedge, why is it occupying the middle of my best flowerbed? Organizing one's plants is not for the softhearted. The collector, always working out how to fit in some new acquisition, has to find out which plants will grow just as well in poor positions, in which case they are unceremoniously moved. No easy living around *here.*

Green Flowers

With the eccentric taste of a typical collector, I find green flowers especially enticing. A well-known gardening dictionary describes *Veratrum californicum* (Zone 5) as "a coarse, perennial herb," with flowers an "off-white, base green." After reading that, who would want to grow it? I must contradict this authority, for the Californian veratrum is a dream of a plant, with great panicles of palest green starry flowers, the color of mint ice-cream, on stout, upstanding, four-foot stems. The bold, immaculately pleated leaves make this veratrum into a personality plant of the first quality. Because they resent disturbance, I am reluctant to divide and replant my veratrums. So in order to supply the rich feeding they demand, I make a trench about four inches deep around the plants in spring; this is then filled up with handfuls of bonemeal and buckets of manure.

Bupleurum angulosum (Zone 6) is a charming small member of the cow parsley family, about fifteen inches high with slender, linear leaves. The

"petals" (which are in fact bracts) are pale jade green, surrounding the true flowers which are tiny and acid yellow—the whole giving the effect of a small green water lily. Acid yellow-green on a much larger scale is found in *B. fruticosum* (Zone 7). As soon as this southern European shrub comes into bloom in late summer you'll recognize it as a relation of Queen Anne's lace by the shape of the flowers. The polished evergreen leaves have a beautiful blue sheen. In Dublin this plant needs a sunny wall, but will stand the hard pruning required to keep it within bounds at the back of the flower border. Many shrubs look incongruous mixed in with perennials, but I consider this bupleurum one of the best, along with buddlejas, fuchsias, and shrub roses.

Astrantia major subsp. *involucrata* 'Shaggy' (Zone 6), unlike the typical greater masterwort, has an outer circlet of unusually large, green-tipped bracts around the central posy of tiny florets, on two- to three-foot stems. I can't understand why this marvelous plant isn't in every garden (climate permitting). It flowers for ages, is lovely for summery arrangements indoors, and is easy in rich, moisture-retentive soil. One point: Propagate it by division; don't let it drop seed, or you'll end up with rogue seedlings—which may or may not be as good— growing in the crown of the parent.

At the opposite end of the scale is obscure little *A. minor* (Zone 6), which you wouldn't notice in a crowd. I suspect nobody likes it but me. The flowers are delicate fairy pincushions on slender,

*Astrantia maxima, a
masterwort from
European meadows,
is as pretty in a vase as
it is in the garden.
It prefers a rich,
retentive soil.*

foot-high stems. In an effort to please this plant, I've tried it in several different places; it is now seeding itself in the peaty raised bed near the oval lawn. (In the wild, apparently, it is found mainly on acid soil.) For those of more sanguinary taste, look for two dark red cultivars of *A. major*, namely 'Hadspen Blood' and the sensational 'Ruby Wedding'. Lastly (I know I'm meant to be discussing green flowers), I particularly like *A. maxima*; this is shorter than *A. major*, but the flowers are large, beautiful, and shell pink. It has a definite preference for a cool spot.

Hacquetia epipactis (Zone 6), a small, shade-loving spring perennial, is by no means a self-important plant, but is nevertheless a quiet masterpiece. The "flowers" are composed of bright green bracts surrounding a cluster of tiny yellow true flowers. It likes humus-rich, moist soil and takes time to settle down after division. You need a group of a plant such as this; a singleton looks rather forlorn.

Hardy Orchids and Orchid Lookalikes

If you examine an individual floret of *Dactylorhiza elata* (Zone 6) you'll notice the flowers are just like an exotic hothouse orchid, the sort that embellished the bosom of an Edwardian lady's dress. The robust marsh orchid—an easy plant, providing you choose a peaty, leaf-moldy, not-too-dry spot—makes a glorious display in early summer of long-lasting

thirty-inch spires of bright rose-purple flowers and mid-green, strap-shaped leaves. *Dactylorhiza maculata* 'Kilmarnock' (Zone 6), is just as nice. It is similar to *D. elata*, but a bit smaller and paler, with spotted leaves and more speckled flowers. My form of *D. foliosa* (Zone 7), the Madeiran orchid, has chubby, clear magenta flowerheads on eighteen-inch stems and shiny green leaves, but I understand the color can be variable.

When happy, dactylorhizas increase quite quickly. Then the time comes when they must be divided—a worrying operation, for the fleshy tubers, like succulent underground fingers, seem so full of life that you hardly dare touch them. Early autumn is the optimum time for division. The clumps separate easily. Each new tuber, with a shiny green snout on top, will still be attached to the old, which shouldn't be removed. Plant them so that the snout is about an inch below the surface, and mark the patch carefully with sur-

PRECEDING

OVERLEAF

The queen of lady's

slippers, Cypripedium

reginae. *Not to be*

given away—it's very

unwise to disturb an

established clump.

RIGHT

There was great

excitement among Irish

gardeners when this

pure white roscoea

seedling turned up in a

Tipperary garden (not

photographed at

Sandford Road).

Undisturbed for the

past eleven years, a

clump of the yellow

lady's slipper orchid

*(*Cypripedium calceo-

lus *var.* pubescens*)*

thrives on the raised

bed in the Sundial

Garden. Large stones

keep the roots cool.

rounding canes. (As with trilliums, a misplaced foot could well finish them off.) These spectacular, vigorous, hardy orchids should only be given to your best friends.

We will gloss over the fate in this garden of the extremely rare British native, *Cypripedium calceolus*, and celebrate instead the continued survival of its American cousin, *C. calceolus* var. *pubescens* (Zone 5). The yellow lady's slipper orchid is a beautiful plant with lemon-yellow pouches finely spotted with maroon inside, and greenish brown sepals and petals, the latter spirally twisted. This grows in a raised bed in sun with added peat.

Cypripedium reginae (Zone 4), another American native and the queen of lady's slippers, is almost too divine a plant to mention, with a delicious rose-pink inflated pouch. Miserly instincts should be allowed to triumph when it comes to cypripediums; in my experience it is very unwise to disturb an established clump.

Roscoeas could almost be described as poor man's orchids, although they are in fact members of the ginger family, the Zingiberaceae, which also includes turmeric and cardamom. With an orchid-like presence, at first sight roscoeas look like choice and difficult plants, which is not by any means the

Helleborus ✕ *niger-cors, a hybrid between the true Christmas rose,* Helleborus niger, *and the Corsican hellebore,* H. argutifolius, *grows in a convenient gap in the paving of the Iris Garden.*

glowing purple flowers in early summer. *Roscoea auriculata* (Zone 6), taller at around two feet, is also rather good, making a refreshing patch of shining green leaves and cool purple flowers in late summer. *Roscoea alpina* (Zone 6) is a somewhat boring plant with small purple flowers. Several roscoeas self-seed, but needless to say this last is the most fecund. It has now been removed to an unsalubrious spot and left to get on with it. There was great excitement in Ireland when a pure white roscoea seedling turned up a few years ago in a Tipperary garden, but with me this thrilling color break hasn't proved a very strong plant.

case. In the front of the border, in part shade and rich humusy soil, *Roscoea cautleoïdes* (Zone 6), from China, multiplies happily, presenting bouquets of exquisite clear lemon flowers in summer from sheaves of shining green leaves. Even better is the form 'Kew Beauty', with larger flowers on shorter stems. Roscoeas have fleshy, brittle rhizomes. Books recommend spring division, but I think autumn is preferable in mild climates since you can see what you're doing and are less likely to stick a fork through the roots. Roscoeas are sensitive to frost, so plant the roots eight inches deep. Mark the position carefully, for growth doesn't start until June, thus causing an annual panic over where they've got to.

There are several more species here and different forms thereof, all valuable, in particular a good form of *R. humeana* (Zone 7), a neat plant with

Hellebores

Hellebores are perhaps the most magical plants I grow. I adore them all. Heaven, for me, would be a large field of rich, retentive soil on a north-facing slope, in which to grow their numerous seedlings to flowering size. But here they must be culled before they smother the parent plants, an almost unbearable operation.

The so-called orientalis hybrids (*Helleborus* ✕ *hybridus* is the appropriate botanical name for this mixed bunch of crossbreeds; Zone 4) have glossy, evergreen, divided leaves, forming a mound about eighteen inches high. Their flowers come in meltingly beautiful colors, ranging from pure white (or the sort of green you see on the walls of 1930s bathrooms) to primrose and lemon, to rosy pink, burgundy, and claret, and to the numerous variations on the theme of murky purple and almost blue-black. The darkest have a silvery, plumlike bloom. Their nodding, cup-shaped flowers are remarkably large, up to three inches in diameter, compared to the usually meek little plants of winter and spring. A further dimension is apparent when you lift up each flower, for they are often exquisitely spotted within, each one unique, sometimes as if with a fine pen dipped in ruby ink, sometimes densely speckled all over in maroon.

From the moment their buds first show color (sometimes before midwinter) they gradually increase in beauty. Even after the flowers are fertilized, as spring turns into summer, their colors dim to beautiful understated hues—old rose and mauvy greens—that remind me of faded dowagers.

The Corsican hellebore, *H. argutifolius* (Zone 7), forms superb mounds of architectural foliage. Semiwoody stems bear handsome trifoliate leaves edged with prickly teeth, and like cool leather to touch. Great trusses of cup-shaped, lime-green flowers on three-foot stems seem luminous from a distance. This hellebore from Corsica and Sardinia prefers plenty of sun and rich, well-drained soil.

Helleborus foetidus (Zone 6) is a somewhat shorter plant; it is often treated as a Cinderella among hellebores, since it will thrive in poorer parts of the garden, gracefully furnishing dry shade. The panicles of flower are set off by palest green bracts, the same color as the tulip-shaped

flowers, which are delicately edged with maroon, in striking contrast to the intense dark green, deeply divided leaves. Although it is commonly known as the stinking hellebore, all I can detect is a faint sour smell when the leaves are crushed.

The ultimate hellebore for the picky collector has to be *H. lividus* (Zone 8–9), a refined, much smaller, and very lovely relation of the Corsican hellebore. The Majorcan hellebore produces gray-green trifoliate leaves, marbled above with silvery green, while underneath each leaflet is flushed smoky-mauve with maroon veins. The apple-green flowers and stems are heavily suffused with purple pink. My plant, from wild-collected seed, is kept in a clay pot in a gritty mixture, well away from trouble, for if *H. argutifolius* is anywhere near they will cross-pollinate, and I want to keep the

Yellow Lenten roses (now very fashionable) flowering with "wooden enemies"— our native wood anemone (Anemone nemorosa).

Helleborus × sternii, *the cross between the Corsican and the Majorcan hellebore.*

tender the plant is likely to be. 'Boughton Beauty' is an excellent cultivar, producing a large crop of seedlings, which warrant careful selection.

The best forms of the Christmas rose, *H. niger* (Zone 4), have sumptuous large white flowers with a central boss of yellow stamens and emerald nectaries, borne on foot-high, maroon-speckled stems above dark evergreen pedate leaves. A lovely thing, but despite all efforts, it never seems happy in my light soil. When crossed with *H. lividus,* the result is *H. × ballardiae* (named in honor of Helen Ballard, who first made this hybrid). This garden hybrid is quite rare and because it's not hardy, I grow it at the foot of a sheltered north-facing wall. Attributes of both parents are displayed by cup-shaped greenish white flowers, flushed with purplish pink, and nicely marbled leaves. More garden worthy is *H. × nigercors* (Zone 7), a cross with *H. argutifolius,* very robust, with huge trusses of scintillating, creamy flowers tinged with luminous green.

Hellebores are among the greediest of plants. When planting, I work in at least two buckets of fresh topsoil mixed with well-rotted manure, garden compost, leaf mold, and bonemeal. To prevent the spread of fungus (one symptom of which is black spotting on the leaves), the old leaves of the orientalis hybrids are cut off in late autumn; in any case the plants look much better at flowering time without their tattered foliage. Never cut off the leaves of *H. argutifolius, H. foetidus,* or *H. lividus*—there'd be nothing left of the plant. All are sprayed with fungicide every two to three weeks from January until April, although this

seed pure. When flowering is well over, it's allowed out for the summer. The cross between these two hellebores, *H. × sternii* (Zone 6 more or less), displays features from both parents in varying proportions. The more pink flush to the flowers, inherited from *H. lividus,* the more

measure is probably not necessary in areas with colder winters. I've noticed that plants in really prime positions—lightly shaded, with a rich root run and no shortage of summer moisture—appear less prone to disease.

Once upon a time I divided my hellebores in early spring, but I've learned (from Elizabeth Strangman and Graham Rice's book *The Gardener's Guide to Growing Hellebores*) that the orientalis hybrids make a lot of root growth in autumn and winter, so early autumn is the optimum moment for this operation. Division involves a bucket of water to wash the roots so that you can see what you're doing, and a sharp kitchen knife. In my experience small pieces establish faster than large sections.

My choice selection of orientalis hybrids includes 'Philip Ballard' (slaty blue-black), 'Blue Spray' (smoky blue-purple), 'Citron' (pale primrose), 'Graigueconna' (variegated, creamy speckled leaves, cream flowers), 'Greencups' (self-explanatory, lovely), 'Günther Jürgl' (double, pale pink, finely spotted), 'Hidcote Double' (found at Hidcote by Graham Thomas, divine, double dirty maroon), 'Rubens' (rich red-purple, large open flowers), and 'Nocturne' (black-purple buds and bracts, deep smoky purple). Before you throw this book at the wall, take heart—there are some good, rapidly improving seed strains available. You can sow seed from a good named cultivar and the results may be as good as the parent.

Hellebore seed should be sown as soon as it is ripe, in pots filled with a gritty mixture. The

When Helleborus lividus, *the Majorcan hellebore, is grown near its Corsican cousin,* H. argutifolius, *they will cross-pollinate with impunity, so I grow mine in a pot in the Alpine House to keep the seed pure.*

shining black seeds are easy to see and should be spaced an inch apart. Top up the pot with one-half inch of grit and leave them outside until germination takes place. The pot should then be moved under well-ventilated glass for protection.

Middle-Aged Roses

Spare a thought for the middle-aged rose. Old-fashioned roses, heavenly as they are, have all the publicity, while some of the roses bred this century are nearly forgotten. 'Mrs. Oakley Fisher', a single hybrid tea bred in Britain in 1921, has soft apricot single blooms in the shape of a Tudor rose. Said to be highly fragrant (I can only detect a faint perfume), she has splendid dark green leaves flushed with red. There is nothing brash about 'Mrs. Oakley Fisher'—one can imagine her namesake drifting around 1920s tea dances or vicarage garden parties, never to be seen without hat or gloves.

There used to be two specimens of 'Mrs. Oakley Fisher' in the red border. But lovely as the flowers are at every stage from bud to hip, I finally decided that apricot was totally inappropriate among all the different reds. They have now been moved to grow beside 'Lady Hillingdon'.

"Reader, I moved it" sounds far too glib a description for what actually happened when 'Mrs. Oakley Fisher' was transplanted. Although the move itself was accomplished in a trice, prior to that three days were spent digging up a colony of pink lily of the valley (*Convallaria majalis* var. *rosea*; Zone 3) to make way for the rose. If you've ever tried to dig up a long-established patch of lily of the valley, you'll know what I mean—it is like trying to unearth a rug of tangled wire, so matted are the roots.

Once the position of a plant starts to annoy me, I itch to move it. Many a rose has been dug up in full flower, carried up the garden, and propped up against a fork to see how it looks. The decision made, the flowers are put in a vase of water, the stems are cut hard back, and any torn roots trimmed. This operation is done at great speed and I try not to imagine what the rose thinks about all this. Early autumn is the prime moment for these garden upheavals—by then I've had a whole summer to be annoyed and can wait no longer, and the soil is nicely warm and moist to aid the plant's recovery.

You may know the celebrated remark about the rose 'Lady Hillingdon'—"She's no good in bed but great against a wall"—made on account of her reputation for being tender. Of similar coloring to 'Mrs. Oakley Fisher', the apricot flowers of this rose are large, semidouble, and fragrant of tea, with plum-colored stems and deep green leaves. The climbing form grown here is excellent on a warm wall, despite the fact that I'm endeavoring to keep it to ten feet (it would prefer to grow to twenty), and it doesn't much like being pruned.

Apricot is a tricky color to cope with. Determined to find suitable planting partners for these two roses, I'm trying blue and white flowers and glaucous and gray foliage. *Bulbinella hookeri* (Zone 8), a New Zealand perennial about one foot high with racemes of starry, egg-yolk-yellow flowers and grassy foliage (rather like a small kniphofia in appearance), is going to be moved to the same bed. Hitherto it has never looked right, no matter where it was placed. Pale orange candelabra primulas should bloom in unison, and the scheme may at last make sense.

There is invariably a domino effect when you move one plant—further reshuffling always seems necessary. On the other side of the path, opposite 'Mrs. Oakley Fisher', was the sweetest little rose, 'Pompon de Paris', in sugar pink—the worst possible near apricot. I would have moved this, too, except the base of the plant was congested with dead growth, so I took cuttings. They were rooted, potted on, and in full flower within a few months.

Many roses in this garden have been propagated by cuttings—not by the traditional method of taking hardwood cuttings in early autumn, but by rooting them in warmth in summer. Young shoots, about five inches long, are taken, trimmed of lower leaves, and inserted firmly around the edge of small pots of peat and sand. These are placed under a bell jar in the greenhouse and kept shaded. For adding to your collection the alternative way, try visiting your friends at the height of the rose season and asking for a few flowering stems: these make ideal cutting material; just nip off the spent flowers.

I think it was E. A. Bowles who couldn't bear watching another gardener planting something, and itched to do it his way. I feel the same about watching people placing cuttings in a pot. Their fingers never seem to firm the cuttings in as well as I'd like. To be sure of making them properly firm, I always sprinkle the pot of cuttings with water, and then lightly press each one in again. And people don't seem to realize that you must always have an *uneven* number of cuttings in the pot; if not, the fairies will get them and the cuttings won't root.

More Roses

'Souvenir du Docteur Jamain', introduced about 1865, is a climbing hybrid perpetual easily kept to about six feet. The flowers are deep port wine, melting into velvety violet-black in the shadows between the petals. It smells just as you think a red rose should, with a fragrance to swoon for. I adore this rose, and feel mean if I don't conduct visitors up the garden to see it. They usually take a tentative sniff, start to turn away, then come back for more, this time sinking their noses deep into the middle of the flower, inhaling great drafts of its languorous scent.

Strong sun shrivels the edges of the petals. Rain turns the flowers into damp crimson paper handkerchiefs. So you need to think carefully about where to position it. I have it growing in the light shade of the 'Bramley' apple. 'Souvenir du Docteur Jamain' is never a mass of flower, but there are few days during the summer on which you cannot find one perfect bloom.

'William Lobb' (1885) has healthy-looking foliage with a bluish tinge and lovely mossy buds, each one covered in velvety green chenille. The fragrant, semidouble, purple blossoms are a picture of faded beauty—mauve, magenta, and pinky-gray all mingled together. It flowers only once, but stays in bloom about six weeks, for the last two of which daily deadheading should take place. 'William Lobb' is a vigorous rose; its prickly stems reach to eight feet when trained to a rustic pole, but I'm now insisting it become more of a bush by pruning it hard to three feet—I saw it treated thus to good effect in a Tipperary garden.

"'Souvenir de Saint Anne's'," remarked Graham Stuart Thomas, when he came here some years ago, "is a rose that should be in every garden." This Irish rose has all the charm of the old-fashioned sorts, without being so prey to blackspot and mildew. The blooms are shell pink

with deeper pink buds, it is never without a flower from May until December, and the leaves are a clean gray-green—a nonpareil of a rose, should you have room for only one.

'Souvenir de Saint Anne's' arose around the turn of the century as a sport from the old Bourbon rose 'Souvenir de la Malmaison', in the Ardilauns' garden, St. Anne's, at Clontarf on the north side of Dublin. Lady Ardilaun jealously guarded her rose, and would only part with a cutting provided the recipient promised never to give a plant away. This lovely rose would never have survived had it not been cherished by Lady Moore, wife of Sir Frederick Moore, onetime director of the Botanic Gardens at Glasnevin. After Lady Ardilaun's death, Phylis Moore gave it to Graham Thomas, who distributed it to the nursery trade in the 1950s.

A sublime little insight into the bitchy world of Edwardian gardening is shown in a letter to Frederick Moore from Miss Ellen Willmott (1858–1934), the celebrated English gardener, renowned for her acerbic views about some of her contemporaries. Having met Lady Ardilaun in France, she wrote that she "was surprised how very little [Lady Ardilaun] knew about plants and gar-

Old-fashioned glass bell jars are in use for most of the year in the greenhouse for rooting cuttings of all sorts, including roses.

dening…but she told me her garden at St. Anne's was quite wonderful." Miss Willmott then added the coup de grâce: "Whatever be the case it is most fortunate that the owner is so completely satisfied."

'Mme Grégoire Staechelin', bred in Spain in 1927, is a vigorous climbing rose. Festooning the wrought iron arches at the end of the garden with voluptuous pink blossoms, showering the path beneath with pink petals, she presents a lavish display in late May, fully two weeks before the main flush of roses begins. She blooms only once, unlike the repeat-flowering 'Climbing Mme Caroline Testout', who drapes herself over a nearby arch, with flowers in similar vein: silver-pink, fragrant, and decadent to the last—the stuff that Ascot hats are made of. Some people might consider that such gorgeous beauties as these mesdames should remain where they belong—on chintz curtains and the tops of chocolate boxes. But for me the pink cabbage rose is the essence of summer.

So full-petaled and so precise is the bowl shape of the flowers of 'Charles de Mills' it is as if you are being presented with a cup of sumptuous, deep purple-red petals, beautifully folded around each other. A neat, bushy rose, easily kept to five feet, this grows near the purple elder *Sambucus nigra* 'Guincho Purple' (Zone 5), cerise crimson *Lychnis* × *walkeri* 'Abbotswood Rose' (Zone 6), and some purple-leaved sedums, in what's known as "No-man's-land"—that forgotten corner which always gets missed at weeding time.

Poor 'Mme Hardy' isn't in a good position: She is in the rain shadow of next door's yew tree, strug-

gling to produce her ravishing, double, fragrant pure white flowers with a bright green eye in the middle; she'll have to be moved again. Sugar-pink 'Hermosa' was transplanted last autumn to the pink border to join 'Louise Odier'; 'Jacques Cartier' likewise. I love 'White Wings' for its single white flowers of great elegance; as the flower matures, the light bronze stamens slowly deepen to crimson. But in this garden its reputation for being a slow starter certainly applies.

Other People's Weeds

Many plants require that their every whim be catered for, but I love those that you can plant and forget. Then up they suddenly pop, smiling from the gravel, the hedge bottom, or a gap in the paving—just the sort of plants for the hopeless gardener, the type who mows the lawn with deep reluctance once a week.

Erigeron karvinskianus (Zone 7) is the sort of plant that would do the gardening for him. A little daisy from Mexico and Central America, less than a foot in height, the flowers open pale pink and deepen as they mature. Charming. It self-seeds madly, and the only reason I can think of why it isn't common is that it looks like such a miserable little creature in a nursery pot that nobody would buy it. On the other hand, given a clay pot, a gritty compost, and full sun, it makes a pretty container plant. It flowers nonstop until frost. It has

OVERLEAF
Don't interplant Cyclamen coum, *as I did, with* Crocus tommasinianus, *because the crocus will swamp it with innumerable seedlings.*

PRECEDING

OVERLEAF

Johnny-jump-up
(Viola tricolor*), the
nicest possible weed,
with flowers in endless
permutations of cream,
yellow, purple, and
mauve, and
Osteospermum 'Irish
Lavender', raised in
Finda Reid's Dublin
garden.*

become naturalized in chinks of the sandstone terrace at Killruddery, Co. Wicklow, one of Ireland's oldest gardens, laid out in the seventeenth century. Gardeners in hotter countries probably consider *E. karvinskianus* a pernicious weed.

Crocus tommasinianus (Zone 5) is frowned on by bulb specialists, for it seeds itself with great abandon, unconcerned about position, and with a special preference for the center of your choicest alpine. No matter, I love it. What more heavenly weed could you get? In February the garden is a radiant sea of pearly lilac. And when the sun shines the pools of color double and treble as thousands of little crocuses open to the warmth. The borders are infested with its corms, and later in the year I'm always digging them up by mistake and crossly throwing them away, forgetting that with each cluster goes a handful of color.

Crocus tommasinianus also promiscuously cross-pollinates other crocuses, and the offspring of these illicit liaisons are usually weeds too. The seedlings that appear among patches of the *tommasinianus* cultivars 'Barr's Purple', 'Ruby Giant' (possibly a hybrid with *C. vernus*), and white 'Albus' (slow to get going) are in various shades of pink. Transplanting them to bloom beside *Cyclamen coum* causes the usual dilemma: pink crocuses, albeit divine next to magenta cyclamen, are certain to cause problems with their innumerable offspring. Imagining great swathes of ruby, amethyst, and purple for the future, I always move them in flower. The irritation of constantly digging them up by mistake is forgotten when the garden transcends itself in spring.

The Labrador violet, once *Viola labradorica*, now known as *Viola riviniana* Purpurea Group (Zone 2), which comes from as far north as Greenland, has rosy-lilac flowers delicately veined inside and dark green kidney-shaped leaves. If you saw this violet all dressed up in a pot at a flower show, you'd think it was a plant to die for. But, unlike some pampered violas such as 'Irish Molly', which has to be grown from cuttings, this is a marvelous weed, self-perpetuating, and with a built-in maintenance clause—you only need to buy it once.

The name pansy (from the French *pensée*) was first used for *Viola tricolor* (Zone 4). Also known as Johnny-jump-up, love-in-idleness, and heart's-ease, this European seaside pansy is the nicest possible weed. The little flowers make you smile, for each has a different face in every combination of yellow, lavender, and purple. I have a fickle attitude toward this viola. Old plants are torn out by the bucketful during the autumn tidy-up to make room for choicer customers, but then all is forgiven during mild spells when the cheeky flowers brave the winter air.

Plants That Need Protection

THE ALPINE HOUSE

Alpine houses exist in Ireland for two reasons. Alpines are frost hardy, but in the wild they are kept dry by a layer of

The Alpine House in January, with Narcissus romieuxii 'Julia Jane' (found by plant collector Jim Archibald in Morocco and named after his daughter). In the wild these daffodils have a wet winter and a hot, dry summer, so I find the bulbs need to be dried off after flowering.

snow (it is not cold but wet that kills them), which also insulates them and keeps them at a constant temperature. Thus certain plants from high altitudes must be protected from our mild wet winters, so my alpine house is fully ventilated at all times. It is shaded from April to September by green net curtaining on the outside. Waist-high staging is covered in a six-inch layer of damp sand in which to plunge the pots. Second, alpine houses also provide excuses for dawdling away whole afternoons, gazing at the plants, doing nothing in particular except occasionally sticking a finger into a pot to see if it wants watering. I grow several plants with a reputation for being difficult.

Primula allionii (Zone 6), for example, comes from almost inaccessible limestone cliffs in the Maritime Alps of France and Italy. It must never have so much as one drop of water on its leaves, so it is safest grown in a clay pot plunged in damp sand; enough moisture reaches the roots through the porous sides of the pot for the dormant plant

The Alpine House in spring.

to thrive. However, when the plants are in full growth, plenty of water is needed, so the pots are soaked for several minutes twice a week or so to within an inch of the rim. Up to a third of the potting compost consists of grit to assist drainage, which must at all times be faultless. Dead leaves encourage rotting and are laboriously removed, using tweezers and a little downward tug; an inadvertent pull the other way and the leaf rosettes fall off. What's more, to prevent a lopsided effect, caused by the plants leaning toward the light, each pot should be given a quarter-turn once a week.

What a rigamarole. If *Primula allionii* flowered in June, I wouldn't bother. But this delicate primrose is a thrilling sight in February and March. The leaf rosettes form immaculate domes, glowing with jewel-like flowers. Depending on the cultivar, the flowers may be from crystalline white through pale pink to various shades of lilac pink, rich crimson, and dark reddish purple. The plants are quite slow growing, and things usually go well for the first few years. But once the plants get to be about five inches across, the trouble starts, and leaf rosettes die off in succession. But *P. allionii* is easy from summer cuttings, so there's no excuse not to have young plants in reserve.

Androsace vandellii (Zone 4), also a member of the primula family, requires similar treatment: perfect drainage, perfect ventilation, no overhead watering at any time, and summer shading. In April tight cushions of little silver leaves are almost hidden by a profusion of exquisite white blossoms. As soon as people see this plant, they immediately give it a pat—it has a magnetic attraction for the human hand.

These two plants undoubtedly need careful cultivation, but at least their requirements are clear. One reads vague instructions for many alpines, such as "Keep dry but not arid in winter" or "Likes a dryish summer." I want specific orders such as "Apply two tablespoons of water every second Saturday," but alas, this can't happen. You have to learn to grow plants in your own unique conditions.

Primula aureata (Zone 4), a Nepalese plant, is perhaps the most ravishing of a diverse and very beautiful genus. In shape and size, it is fairly similar to our native Irish primrose, *P. vulgaris*. The leaves are densely coated in farina, as if powdered in silver-gilt dust, and the flowers are pale yellow shading to a deeper eye. I water the pots from above, but water is never allowed to spoil their gilded leaves. I like this primrose so much that I normally keep ten or so pots of it in the alpine house, growing in a compost of one-third each leaf mold, peat-based ericaceous compost, and grit. I administer several doses of liquid fertilizer in late summer. Are you wondering why this heavenly plant is so rarely seen? Hot summers are fatal; it insists on that most elusive growing condition of all—year-round coolth.

In addition to primroses and their relatives, the alpine house always contains a few favorites: oreganoes, several cyclamen, *Narcissus romieuxii* 'Julia Jane' (a January-flowering pale lemon hooped petticoat daffodil), *Campanula zoysii* (Zone 6), *Physoplexis comosa* (Zone 6), rhodohypoxis, pleiones, and various New Zealand clematis, including *C. × cartmanii* 'Joe' (see page 82). But the majority of the plants are just passing through, either being propagated or being hardened off, and often just in intensive care.

One major surprise has been the success of the sand plunge as a rooting medium. Many's the time a plant has been saved by snatching a bit off and stuffing this "slip" into the sand. The sand must hold just the right amount of moisture, for all manner of plants have rooted here, whether they be shrub, herb, or alpine. The cuttings can be watered easily if required—I can't miss noticing them on my way through to the potting shed.

THE POTTING SHED

Bell jars and cloches, flowerpots from clay antiques to modern plastic, seed trays and stakes, sieves both large and small, buckets of leaf mold and limestone, a basket of broken crocks for drainage, pencils all in need of sharpening, ties, polyethylene bags, odd lengths of wire and string, containers of dried blood lidded to keep out flies, pliers and paintbrushes, gloves without thumbs, and seeds from the year before last—the miscellaneous paraphernalia of the potting shed consists mostly of things that *might* come in useful.

And a special fern. There is no other place exactly suitable for *Cheilanthes eatonii* (Zone 6), one of the resurrection ferns from North America. It requires low humidity, good ventilation, and a free draining compost. Its fronds, seemingly cut out of silver plush, are irreparably damaged by water splashes, therefore the greenhouse and alpine house are out of bounds.

Nobody knows exactly what goes on in the potting shed, but doubtless I'm very busy and mustn't be disturbed. The potting bench, backed by a low sunny window, is ideal for leaning on. At the sound of approaching footsteps, flowerpots are noisily moved around to give the impression of work in progress.

The potting shed window overlooks a small tiled area. This is a sort of shunting yard for plants—they're on the way to be propagated, hardened off, or given away. New arrivals await a decision about where they should be planted. This lightly shaded, airy spot is the permanent home of *Soldanella carpatica, S. pindicola, S. austriaca*, and *S. minima* (Zone 5–6), choice, spring-flowering plants with rounded leathery leaves from the Alps, Carpathians, and Balkans. The flowers are fragile, delicately fringed bells, whose colors range from violet to rosy-lilac and white. Soldanellas are often accused of not flowering because the flowerbuds, formed in early winter, have been eaten by slugs. A table, each of its legs immersed in a dish of water, now supports the collection. Slugs can't swim; unless they learn to fly, or hitchhike on another plant, they won't get my soldanellas. Long ago soldanellas were called moonworts—why did they abandon this lovely name?

THE GREENHOUSE

Just a few steps from the alpine house is the greenhouse. Despite drips from numerous leaks, unex-

The national flower of Chile, Lapageria rosea, *was a picture of misery when grown outdoors. Now it flourishes in a pocket of lime-free soil in the greenhouse.*

plained drafts, and a wooden staging teetering on the brink of collapse, my frost-free greenhouse allows me to enjoy a whole new world of plants.

The anonymous pericallis (page 90) and *Jasminum polyanthum* (page 24) have already been mentioned, so I must now tell you about another honorary resident of the greenhouse, namely *Lapageria rosea* (Zone 9). This aristocrat among climbers was named for Napoleon's wife, the Empress Joséphine Tascher de La Pagerie, and is the national flower of Chile. The twining, wiry stems, bearing dark evergreen leathery leaves, weave their way up the wires on the greenhouse wall, always turning away from the sun and trying to hide in the shade. Sumptuous, nodding, deep rose bells, mottled light pink within, cool and sensuous to the touch, appear almost throughout the year, with the greatest flush in autumn. Their pollen is pale cream. The empress's namesake grows in a large pocket of lime-free, humus-rich soil, because she doesn't thrive for long in a pot. This plant is easy but slow from seed. I am forever having arguments with people who inform me that their lapageria grows outdoors—as well it may—but existing and flourishing are two quite different states. Mine was a picture of misery outside.

There are several South African plants growing in pots on the staging: bulbs, including cyrtanthus, veltheimias, lachenalias, and various tulbaghias; and sweet-scented pelargoniums, my particular favorites being the so-called rose geranium (a hybrid of *Pelargonium graveolens*) and 'Mabel Grey', which has leaves intensely fragrant of lemon. The perfume

of the tender *Rhododendron* 'Lady Alice Fitzwilliam' permeates the air in spring; her straggly habit is controlled by pruning a few of the stems each year after flowering. Certain salvias are also regulars, such as *Salvia buchananii* (Zone 9), with tubular flowers of rich rose purple, like the plush velvet of cinema seats, and vivid blue-flowered *S. guaranitica* (Zone 8), which flowers much earlier under glass.

The rest of the plants in the greenhouse are an itinerant population, mostly in the process of propagation. Congestion point is reached every April, when you can't move without knocking something over.

Invaluable for rooting cuttings are three old-fashioned bell jars in use for most of the year. The high season for taking cuttings is late August/early September, which allows time for them to be well rooted before winter.

Poppies

Have you ever watched an opium poppy unfold? The tightly crushed petals swell with inner force, and off pops the bud casing. The new petals, all wrinkly and crumply, shake themselves silky smooth. The moment the flower is fully open, cruising bumblebees dive into the middle, clambering tipsily among the stamens, wallowing in the pollen. There is a moment's furious buzzing; the flower vibrates with frenzied activity; and pollination has taken place—a little drama that happens very early on summer mornings.

*This prickly poppy (*Argemone *species) is perennial, long-lived, and self-seeding in poor soil in sun.*

For a few weeks I adore opium poppies (*Papaver somniferum*; Zone 4). Their vibrant colors introduce fresh sparkle to the borders. And every year I marvel at the brilliant design of their pearly, gray-green seedheads, and wish I were a silversmith making elegant cruets of silver seedhead peppers and salts, reclining on silvered leaves. Then suddenly I've had enough of opium poppies, as their fading stems start toppling over, and I crossly yank them out, all except those wanted for seed. Only then do I remember what bullies they are, adept at smothering smaller neighbors with their cabbagey leaves.

Your own seed strain of opium poppies is remarkably simple to organize. I inherited washy lilac poppies, but by marking any slight variants—lighter, darker, or faintly pink—with a cane and letting only these drop their seed, I now have cherry-red, rich purple, and rose-pink, and, from seed mailed from Australia, a pristine white.

Meconopsis quintuplinervia (Zone 8), which prompted Reginald Farrer's remark about "myriad dancing lavender butterflies," comes from Tibet and China. Tuffets of basal leaves are clothed in stiff, russety hairs. The solitary, nodding, four-petaled flowers are borne on fifteen-inch stems. I am honored that this heavenly poppy graces my garden, growing in one of the peat beds near the Oval Lawn. The plant spreads slowly by underground runners, which are easily detached for propagation. The sort of plant you can never rely on—I regularly transplant a spare piece to a different spot. But the harebell poppy has a mind of its own, and insists on doing well only in its original position. My plants have never set seed.

The most ethereal annual poppies were given to me as Cedric Morris's "Fairy Poppies" (now marketed, I believe, as 'Fairy Wings' or 'Mother of Pearl'). Their flowers are composed of petals gossamer-fine in muted hues of peach, dusty pink, and smoky grays and mauves, some with a picotee edge, some traced with lines of infinite delicacy, others with petals like shot silk, the color changing with the angle from which you view the flower.

More than twenty years ago, I rashly grew some Welsh poppies (*Meconopsis cambrica*; Zone 6). from seed. There's no controlling these Celts— they seed precisely where they fancy, usually into the center of your choicest specimen. But their yellow flowers vividly illuminate a dull corner in dry shade by the yard gate, dotted through the green fronds of the male fern (*Dryopteris filix-mas*; Zone 2), the most forgiving fern for such a position. Welsh poppy seedlings, wary from years of being hunted by gardeners, are masters of disguise. A sharp knife is necessary for dislodging their obstinate white carrotty roots.

Double Welsh poppies (*M. cambrica* 'Flore Pleno') are considerably more sober in their habits. They seed themselves mildly, and come roughly 70 percent double in this garden. Singles must be taken out the instant they reveal themselves. The double flowers range from the chemical brilliance of a fizzy orange drink to a very-good-taste light yellow. Deadheading promotes a long season of flower.

Now for the extravaganza of early summer, as the Oriental poppies (*Papaver orientale*; Zone 3) enter the garden scene. The huge, flamboyant flowers are composed of glistening petals surrounding a velvety knob that luxuriates in the middle. My favorite is 'Cedric's Pink', with flowers knicker-pink like twenties underclothes, seductively blotched with purple at the base of each petal. 'Black and White' I think far more dashing, and more Persil-white, than 'Perry's White', which is in reality a disappointingly pale pink.

From the celandine poppy *(Stylophorum diphyllum;* Zone 5) of spring to the stately plume poppy (*Macleaya cordata*; Zone 3) and prickly poppy (*Argemone* species) of summer, the family Papaveraceae leads us at last to the queen of all the poppies, the California tree poppy (*Romneya coulteri;* Zone 7). Both books on shrubs and books on herbaceous perennials insist on including *Romneya*, which is understandable. The voluptuous flowers of this glorious poppy have silky white crinkled petals surrounding a golden aureole of stamens, and a peculiar, pleasing fragrance. It was eight years before my specimen settled down, upon which it set off in all directions. Each winter I cut it to the ground, so it flowers at the ideal height for close contemplation. You'd think the California tree poppy could be simply propagated by potting up suckers. Not

so. The suckers will give all the appearance of healthy root growth, when in fact they're just sitting and thinking about it. Don't disturb the pots for at least six months.

Prickles, Thistles, and Spikes

Some gardeners seem almost to see with their fingers, they itch to handle plants. One doesn't actually have to *touch* plants to gain a sense of their tactile quality, although the silky leaves of such plants as *Convolvulus cneorum* and silver velvet of *Salvia argentea* are irresistible to stroke. I relish the contrast of plants that form soothing friendly mounds, like artemisias, lavender, and santolina, with spiky-looking customers that you almost need a suit of armor to approach.

Concentration is required when weeding in the vicinity of *Aciphylla scott-thomsonii* (Zone 7). The foliage is composed of vicious, five-pronged, gray-green scimitars with tips like sharpened steel. The three-foot-diameter basal rosette makes a wonderful, year-round architectural feature. When the plant finally builds up enough energy to bloom, you'll recognize it as the most formidable member of the parsley family: Greeny-yellow umbels of flowers, barricaded by deadly thorns, are borne on eight-foot stems. *Aciphylla scott-thomsonii* comes from the cool mountain ranges of New Zealand and doesn't enjoy hot, dry summers—humid Dublin is much to its liking. My plant acts as a vegetable sentry near the front gate.

Acanthus dioscoridis var. *perringii* (Zone 8) is a classy, small acanthus, madly spiny all over. It may not be as imposing as its larger relations, but makes up for it by lavish production of two-foot spikes of prickly, deep purple-pink flowers. Just to think about deadheading it makes my fingers feel sore. It is growing in two places (unintentionally in this case): in full sun on a raised bed and also in gravel. Like all members of the genus, once planted it's there for life; efforts to move an acanthus are usually futile as it regenerates from the roots.

I also once purchased the variegated *Acanthus spinosus* 'Lady Moore' (Zone 6), more out of respect for the great gardener she was than for love of the plant. It is now officially banished, though the occasional shoot is always there to remind me of its presence. Agreed, the spring foliage, predominantly cream at this stage, is pleasant enough, but the mature leaves are far too pallid and sickly-looking for me. *Acanthus mollis* 'New Zealand Gold', a recent arrival, is now being evaluated; so far the large, glossy leaves are cool golden-green; rather nice.

The brook thistle, *Cirsium rivulare* (Zone 5), nothing like so prickly, is usually only recommended for wild gardens. But *C. rivulare* f. *atropurpureum* is a handsome, first-class thistle with a nonstop supply of deep crimson thistly flowers throughout summer. The four-foot stems don't need staking; it isn't invasive; you can leave it in the same position for years; it is a pleasant addition to any color scheme. Put it on your list.

This viciously spiky New Zealander Aciphylla scott-thomsonii *acts as vegetable sentry near the front gate. Although it looks more like a plant of the desert, it comes from mountain areas and dislikes hot, dry conditions.*

Eryngium alpinum (Zone 3) is the beauty of the sea hollies. No less than four different forms grow here, all part of an attempt to find the elusive cultivar 'Slieve Donard' (named for the renowned nursery in Northern Ireland), which is said to have the frilliest, laciest, largest, most silvery-blue ruff surrounding the central flower cone. These various forms differ slightly in size, but all sparkle in the sun with an equally marvelous metallic sheen. At about thirty inches tall, this sea holly needs light staking (a metal hoop is ideal) and full sun to remind it of home in the high alpine meadows. Occasional seedlings turn up.

Visitors never stop remarking on *Eryngium bourgatii* 'Oxford Blue' (Zone 5), a wonderful small thistlelike plant, attractive even out of flower, with dark green leaves conspicuously veined in silver. The intense silvery-blue flowers are much longer lasting than those of *E. alpinum* and the eighteen-inch flower stems are washed in violet. It needs full sun and is easy from seed but it doesn't transplant well unless at the seedling stage.

Primroses

If you go down to the woods today, the primroses won't be there. At least they won't be exactly where you remembered them. They will have seeded themselves on to fresh ground, further up the bank, or down the ditch, or into the woods. *Primula vulgaris* (Zone 4) and its cultivars refuse to thrive for long in the same position, and the uncanny thing about them is that even if you change the soil and replant them in the same spot, they seem to know. They cannot be fooled. In my experience—and this goes for all members of the genus *Primula*—they need regular division (every two years at a minimum) and replanting in fresh topsoil mixed with crumbled old manure and bonemeal, in a *completely different* position.

The most pernickety, and needless to say the most enchanting, are the old doubles, such as 'Alba Plena' and 'Lilacina Plena', in white and mauve respectively. I've had square yards of these in the past, and brushed aside all mention of their tricky reputations. You may know the rest of the story: First the plants look a bit pinched, then the group gets smaller, and finally an irreversible dwindle sets in. But take heart—the primroses can be rescued if dug up and replanted somewhere else.

Primula vulgaris subsp. *sibthorpii* from the Balkans seems more reliable than most with a generous supply of pretty mauve-pink flowers. 'Guinevere', distinguished by purple-bronze leaves and lilac-pink flowers, was raised in Ireland around 1930. 'Lady Greer', another old Irish cultivar, has fragile-looking polyanthus-type pale yellow flowers but a great will to live and increase. The rare 'Tipperary Purple' is a reddish violet Jack-in-the-green, with each flower set in a leafy green ruff. Double blues are very trying, usually going into an early decline, but the single 'Blue Riband', in purple-blue, is an obliging grower. 'Wanda' is the popular old primrose you used to see in cottage gardens, by the path to the front door, making chains of vivid purple-red with golden alyssum and mauve aubrieta.

The cowslip, *Primula veris* (Zone 4), is another plant that likes to move around. The name arose from "cow slip" (from the Old English *cu*, cow, and *slyppe*, slime), from the notion that one would only take root in a meadow where a cow had lifted its tail. You don't go out and buy cowslips. You wait and see. You are honored if they turn up. Try fresh soil from an uncultivated field and a vintage cowpat.

Primroses should be divided in late May, when there are a million other gardening jobs competing for time; autumn division means less of a show the following spring. Don't worry if the primroses look wretched after replanting—they will revive in late summer.

Snowdrops

For the frustrated collector, there's nothing to beat snowdrops (*Galanthus* species). These small bulbs, mostly flowering in late winter and early spring, are natives of western Europe to the Iranian Caucasus and the Caspian Sea. There's no garden too overcrowded to fit in another snow-drop; and, like other addicts, the collector needs a regular fix—early in the year there's little around by way of a flowery intoxicant. The minute differences between one snowdrop and another make for fasci-nating discussion with other galanthophiles; com-parison of green markings on the inner or outer petals, the size of flowers or leaves, or the exact the way the leaves emerge from the bulb (often a clue to which species the snowdrop belongs) all make good diversions for an unsocial season.

If you love great sheets of the common snow-drop, *Galanthus nivalis* (Zone 4), whose pure white flowers and blue-green leaves are radiant under a low spring sun, the next stage is to become capti-vated by the niceties of some other species and cul-tivars. There are around fifty different snowdrops in my garden, but if I could grow only one, it would have to be 'S. Arnott', a snowdrop of singular qual-ity. As petals open in the sun or a warm room, they are voluptuously curved, symmetrical, beautifully poised, and faintly fragrant of honey. It is an easy doer and increases well. 'Magnet' can be immedi-ately recognized by its unusually long, graceful flower stalks, so the flowers quiver in each little breeze, 'Tiny' is indeed very small. The outer petals of 'Viridapicis' are washed in green at the tips—this is a much easier snowdrop than 'Pusey Green Tip', a double that refuses to flourish.

Other doubles include the old *G. nivalis* 'Flore Pleno', a pleasant enough little bulb, but the Irish double, 'Hill Poë', is superior by far, having engagingly plump flowers with five outer petals

(three is the norm) and a tightly frilled green and white middle. 'Lady Elphinstone', a troublesome double, is quite special when thriving, as her inner petals form yellow petticoats, but if she's in a sulk, these are green. Search also for 'Cordelia' and 'Jacquenetta', two scarce doubles with immaculate central rosettes of green.

'Merlin', considered by some to be a hybrid of *G. elwesii*, is a snowdrop as magical as its name: beautiful large flowers open to display inner petals almost entirely green, rimmed with a neat white picotee. The species *G. elwesii* (Zone 6), a native of the Balkans and western Turkey, is distinguished by its telling leaves, light blue-green and up to an inch wide. Gardening books seldom mention how decorative broad swathes of snowdrop foliage can be on naked earth, particularly for places unno-ticed in summer, such as the back of the border.

Galanthus ikariae subsp. *ikariae* (Zone 6), from the Aegean Islands, Turkey, and the Caucasus, is distinct with broad, shining, bright green leaves. It is a good snowdrop for starting a collection, as the foliage makes it instantly recognizable.

Galanthus reginae-olgae (Zone 7) is very similar to the common snowdrop, except that it provides an unexpected treat by flowering in autumn. Its Mediterranean origins suggest a warmer position than most, so I have it growing in a sunny, well-drained raised bed. Despite nourishing additions of leaf mold, it doesn't increase as fast as I'd like.

Among oddities, 'Mrs. Backhouses's Spectacles', an elegant snowdrop with extra-long, slender outer petals, must be grown for its name alone.

If I could grow only one snowdrop, it would have to be Galanthus *'S. Arnott', a snowdrop of singular quality.*

'Boyd's Double' is a miffy monstrosity, apparently in the last stages of virus disease, while 'Virescens', in which the petals are splashed with green, is nice and healthy looking. Sadly, my 'Mighty Atom', aptly named because the flowers are very large for the size of the plant, seems to have disappeared for good. 'Scharlockii', by no means a strong grower here, is a dear little thing; each flower has two long, erect bracts that look just like a donkey's ears.

If you've had no success with snowdrops (assuming your climate is suitable), it's almost certainly because you planted the dry bulbs in autumn—in which case their pathetic display is enough to put you off forever. But if transplanted in growth, "in the green," as they say, either in flower or just after, they settle in immediately. Snowdrops do a lot of growing between flowering and dying down. And this transplanting time not only suits the snowdrop but also suits the gardener—you can see exactly where you are putting them.

Snowdrops prefer moist but well-drained, humus-rich soil in dappled shade. You can fit them in under deciduous trees or among herbaceous plants, in fact anywhere that doesn't bake dry in summer. Choice singletons may be guarded in raised beds until the bulbs increase.

A close eye should be kept on a collection of snowdrops. Go round at flowering time and take immediate action if they're not as good as last year. Say you're dividing a fist-sized clump. Make a hole about a foot in diameter; fill it up with sieved leaf mold, fresh topsoil, and bonemeal; divide the bulbs into groups of two or three (or singles if you're dealing with something special), and plant them about four inches apart. Water, label, and be sure to mark the position carefully—it's impossible to remember exactly where you've planted them.

Lastly, you must try snowflakes. *Leucojum vernum* (Zone 5), the spring snowflake, is a close relative of the snowdrop. In bloom in late January in Dublin, with nodding flowers like glistening little white lampshades, it is brilliantly designed to withstand lashing winter rain, and has shiny dark green leaves. Each pointy petal has a green spot (yellowish in the variety *carpathicum*). They appear to do better after a wet summer and enjoy cooler, moister parts of the garden with plenty of added humus. Whenever I've divided them they've taken a season or two to settle down.

Some Plants Hard to Come By

Maddening as it is to read about plants that are difficult to get, if you don't hear about these plants, there'll be no demand, and they'll sink even deeper into obscurity. The following are all easy, all hardy at least to Zone 6, and deserving of a wider audience.

Lavandula × intermedia 'Hidcote Giant' (Zone 5) is one such (not to be confused with the well-known *L. angustifolia* 'Hidcote.'). When I first grew this lavender, I couldn't quite see the point of it. Taller and less neat in habit than most, it has the purple flowers and felty gray leaves typical of the genus. But the great value of this lavender is that it goes on and on flowering right into autumn, when others have packed up for the season. Every year replacement cuttings are rooted, but I cannot bear to take out the original plant, still a grand old lady of the garden, although rather lopsided with age. It grows by the alpine house door, supplying endless bunches of aromatic flowers, to be crushed and sniffed in passing.

I can't imagine why the European *Geranium argenteum* (Zone 6), one of the gems of a marvelous race, is uncommon. It sets seed. The seed comes up. It is comparatively hardy. It is long lived. It is undeniable lovely. I cannot see what the problem is, except that *G. argenteum* is admittedly too choice to treat in the careless fashion afforded to many hardy geraniums—it couldn't, for example, be expected to survive in the middle of the herbaceous border. No competition in a sunny

raised bed is required for this alpine, rosette-forming perennial up to six inches high, with deeply cut, silvery-silky leaves and pale pink flowers, the petals finely veined in maroon. *Geranium argenteum* 'Lissadell' (another relic from the long-gone nursery near Sligo), in which the flowers are light reddish magenta, is just as desirable.

But I think I know why *Geranium* 'Ann Folkard' isn't that common: Propagation must be done by division, or by chubby spring cuttings that include portions of root; but nurserymen don't like to disturb the plant's roots because there's not much of them. 'Ann Folkard' is the result of a mixed marriage between Caucasian *Geranium psilostemon* (Zone 6) and Himalayan *Geranium procurrens* (Zone 7). This stunningly good plant inherits the

On the edge of a sunny raised bed, Geranium argenteum *(right) and* Geranium argenteum *'Lissadell', bred at Sir Josslyn Gore-Booth's celebrated nursery in County Sligo.*

best features of both: magenta flowers and naughty black eyes from the former, and wandering ways from the latter. But whereas *G. procurrens* is a rampant spreader, 'Ann Folkard' is all tidied away below ground again in winter. It is superlative when scrambling through nearby plants.

Pennisetum orientale (Zone 7) is relatively scarce. I have learned, the hard way, that this grass dislikes interference; autumn division is inevitable death, and even spring divisions look woebegone until nursed in a warm greenhouse. Every spring I think *P. orientale* has "died on me." This Irish gardening remark was succinctly described by E. A. Bowles as "that mild reproach and suggestion of wilful suicide…which so neatly lays the blame on the plant." But after twelve years in the same sharply drained sunny place, *P. orientale* has revived to present each August a ravishing display of fluffy, silvery-mauve flowerheads on two-foot stems, like soft hairy caterpillars to the touch. Betty Farquhar, a special gardening friend of mine in Tipperary, who is now 94, once described the flowerheads as "silver bees." Now she tells me that she said nothing of the sort—but to me, "silver bees" they'll remain.

Lastly I must mention *Omphalodes cappadocica* 'Starry Eyes' (Zone 6), a dear little plant that turned up in Ireland. The species itself is a small, evergreen, creeping perennial with sparkling blue flowers in spring that is happy in not-too-dry shade. 'Starry Eyes' differs by having each petal evenly ribboned in pale pinky-mauve. Very pretty. Very distinct. Charles Nelson, the taxonomist at the Botanic Gardens, Glasnevin, Dublin, made its distribution possible. He gave it to Molly Sanderson in Northern Ireland, with instructions not to give it away. True gardener that she is, when I visited her for lunch I was presented with a piece.

Some Shade Lovers

My gardening nightmare of the year recurs every February, and takes place in the apple bed. All manner of spring delights, shaded by an elderly 'Bramley' apple, grow in this bed. Here, when the first weeding of the year takes place, each footstep means potential heartbreak, threatening to squash the tender snouts of trilliums, erythroniums, Solomon's seals, podophyllums, disporums, uvularias, the succulent, uncurling stems of wood anemones, and the vulnerable fat noses of hostas. Of course I can see such plants as hellebores, pulmonarias, and primroses, and the positions of plants still below ground are flagged by numerous marker canes. But weeding this bed is more a ballet dance of bad temper than a soothing pastime, as my boot—with a sickening scrunch—descends on yet another unseen, juicy shoot.

I'm waiting for the toothworts (*Cardamine* species, formerly *Dentaria*) to receive proper recognition in gardening circles. Agreed, *C. hirsuta* is a sneaky little brute of a weed, but other species are most desirable for their early flowering, not least because their colors include pink,

Anemone nemorosa
'Green Fingers' is an
interesting variant on
our native wood
anemone. The center of
the flower looks like lit-
tle tufts of parsley.
Propagate by division
after flowering.

April. *Cardamine heptaphylla* (Zone 6) is slightly taller, with more erect stems and white flowers, while *C. enneaphyllos* (Zone 5) has creamy-yellow flowers in nice contrast to the young bronze leaves. Several others here include a good, pale violet form of *C. pentaphyllos*, which I like so well it's in five different spots. Divide the odd-looking, whitish, rhizomatous roots in autumn.

Pachyphragma macrophyllum (Zone 6), from the Caucasus and northeastern Turkey, is another member of the Brassicaceae and is perhaps more neglected. It has clusters of pristine white little flowers that present a lacy effect above the glossy, bright green rounded leaves. This plant makes good groundcover for shade, begins to flower with the snowdrops, is still pottering on in May, and is especially good planted near deep purple hellebores. Agreed, it's not a major star, but it well deserves a place in the chorus. Propagate it by spring division.

The lungworts (*Pulmonaria* species) are small, early-flowering perennials with the typical rough-to-touch leaves of the borage family (Boraginaceae). *Pulmonaria officinalis* (Zone 6) is the common, well-loved old garden plant, with heart-shaped spotted leaves and pink-and-blue flowers at the same time. *Pulmonaria angustifolia* (Zone 3) has plain green, unspotted leaves and vivid blue flowers. *Pulmonaria saccharata* (Zone 3) and its cultivars are often so spotted they are frosted silver all over. *Pulmonaria longifolia* (Zone 6) has long, narrow leaves, prominently spotted in white. All are easily grown in part or full shade, in moist, humus-rich

mauve, and purple instead of the more usual yellow and blue of spring. Cardamines can be so conveniently fitted in among shrubs or later perennials; they seem happy anywhere except driest shade, although in the wild they are usually found in damp, mountain woodlands.

Cardamine pentaphyllos (Zone 6) has light green divided leaves and clusters of lilac-pink flowers on one-foot stems from February to late

soil. The moment I plant a new pulmonaria, I'm wondering how soon I can divide it into a large patch—this is much more telling than one little waif marooned in a sea of soil.

Pulmonarias are in fashion, so the number of tempting cultivars is increasing. Among the best are *P. longifolia* 'Bertram Anderson', with handsome, narrow leaves, conspicuously spotted in white and azure blue flowers; *P. rubra* 'David Ward' (Zone 6), with leaves beautifully variegated in cream and light green and brick-red flowers; 'Mrs. Kittle', a little doll of a pulmonaria, with flowers a pale gray-blue, lovely with smoky mauve hellebores; 'Roy Davidson', with narrow, spotted leaves, and flowers of pure light blue; 'Leopard', with spotted leaves, and crimson flowers; and *P. saccharata* 'Dora Bielefeld', with pale green, spotted leaves and true pink flowers.

The fleeting, cup-shapèd, pale pink flowers of the Himalayan mayapple, *Podophyllum hexandrum* (Zone 6), open when the young leaves are just pushing through the soil. At this stage the leaves are like shiny, half-open parasols: when fully unfurled they are deeply lobed and heavily blotched in dark chocolate. The large fruits, similar to plum tomatoes, appear in autumn. Podophyllums are precisely the sort of plant I shouldn't be growing in dry Dublin; they are thus particularly attractive. *Podophyllum peltatum* (Zone 4), from North America, grows nearby, its white flowers hidden beneath the leaves. *Podophyllum versipelle* (syn. *P. mairei*; Zone 7), from China and Tibet, has to date only sent up

one colossal leaf—may the slug who severed this at soil level go to purgatory.

Uvularia grandiflora (Zone 3), from eastern and central North America, is an appealing woodlander, with nodding bell-shaped flowers, each bright yellow petal curled like a soft ringlet, borne on arching two-foot stems in late spring. The fresh green leaves are perfoliate (that is, they are joined at the base, so it looks as if each leaf is

Beautiful shade lovers, the erythroniums (commonly known as dog's-tooth violets or trout lilies) are mulched annually with leaf mold and divided occasionally just after flowering.

Uvularia grandiflora, a North American woodlander, grows in the shade of the 'Bramley' apple. Bucketfuls of humus are worked into the soil during occasional division and replanting.

pierced by the stem). In *U. perfoliata* (Zone 4), the leaves are more obviously perfoliate, the stems are shorter, and the flowers appear slightly later. And in this case they are light yellow. These two pretty and indispensable shade lovers enjoy liberal additions of humus during autumn division.

A colony of autumn-flowering *Cyclamen hederifolium* (Zone 6) grows in a small raised bed built around the trunk of the 'Bramley'. Despite being hard pruned into an umbrella shape, the tree produces a heavy crop of cookers, the best possible sort for apple pies.

A second performance of the snout-and-boot ballet takes place as *Arisaema candidissimum* (Zone 7) emerges in June. From sinister snouts, mottled in maroon, arise hooded white flowers, beautifully striped in candy pink. The large, three-lobed leaves sometimes form umbrellas over the flowers. The tubers don't flower until they are two inches or so in diameter, and should be planted six inches deep to protect them from frost. Numerous small bulbs of *Corydalis solida* (see page 87), snowdrops, and crocuses are growing on top of the arisaemas. Roscoeas (see page 122) never appear until June, and also lend themselves for overplanting with bulbs.

Species Peonies

The first mistake I made with a peony was due to shaky geography. *Paeonia cambessedesii* (Zone 7) comes from the Balearic Islands, to which I'd never been.

The intriguing cowls of Arisaema candidissimum *(a Chinese jack-in-the-pulpit) don't appear till June, so mark the position carefully to prevent accidental disturbance.*

Assuming that these islands consisted mostly of sea and sand, I prepared a compost consisting largely of gravel. The plant never flowered. Lesson number one: All peonies like rich living.

This provoked the second mistake: in a subsequent fit of generosity to a Chinese peony, *P. obovata* var. *alba* (Zone 5), I covered the crown so deep with a crumbly mulch of topsoil, compost, and manure that the plant was smothered to death. Lesson number two: The crown of a peony should not be covered with more than an inch of soil.

Paeonia cambessedesii has metallic, sea-green leaves. The flower stalks and the backs of the leaves are washed in crimson. The fugitive, single, rose-pink flowers appear in early May but the foliage of this wondrous plant provides a long season of beauty. No more than fifteen inches tall, it is suitable for a sunny raised bed and also good in a terra-cotta

Paeonia cambessedesii is now very rare in the wild. Plants in Dublin gardens are descended from one that came direct from Majorca a century ago.

pot. *Paeonia obovata* var. *alba* has single, pure white, equally short-lived flowers—the petals glisten in the sun. The plant is so beautiful that I wouldn't care if it flowered only for a day. The navy blue fertile seeds are mixed with the infertile red ones. Garden visitors are invited to help themselves, provided they can tell me correctly which is which. Both these peonies are easy to raise from seed.

One of the lesser-known species is *Paeonia mascula* subsp. *russii* (Zone 8). My specimen was grown from seed collected in Sardinia. Purple-tinged young leaves and satin-petaled, deep rose-pink single flowers with palest yellow stamens are an opulent sight in April. This peony requires a warm, well-drained position.

Paeonia mlokosewitschii (Zone 4), from the Caucasus, is inexplicably difficult to find. The only reason I can think of is that it doesn't set seed—with me at any rate, although it always seems to be listed in seed exchanges. And, of course, a peony owner is never in a hurry to dig one up to give away—nobody enjoys the sensation of chopping yet another fleshy, fat root in two. The emerging shoots—which are a downy, dusky purple—look succulent enough to eat (steamed, perhaps, with hollandaise sauce, but don't be tempted—peonies are poisonous). The flowers, composed of rounded silky, lemon-yellow petals surrounding a golden powder-puff of stamens, are offset by grayish-green leaves; their scent is impossible to put a name to.

Paeonia tenuifolia (Zone 4), also from the Caucasus, is instantly recognized by its finely dissected leaves. Under eighteen inches tall, this nice, tidy little peony is very scarce in our gardens. The flowers are deep crimson and the stamens yellow. I don't understand why *P. tenuifolia* should be so scarce, as it increases rather well at the root. The double form is a recent acquisition, and the pink 'Rosea' is on my wanted list. *Paeonia veitchii* var. *woodwardii* (Zone 4), from China, has pale pink flowers and, unlike most herbaceous peonies, whose foliage becomes messy by late summer, its leaves remain in good condition. (In colder climates, of course, herbaceous peony foliage remains attractive throughout the summer, finally taking on rich tints in autumn.) It is both easy to grow and easy from seed. Unlike all the peonies mentioned above, this does nicely in light shade.

The Sundial Garden

This little garden, so called for want of a better name, is enclosed on all four sides: by the garden walls, iron trelliswork, and the rose and clematis arcade. In the center is an almost square raised bed, built out of old bricks, surrounding a circular graveled area with a sundial in the middle. It is in sun for much of the day.

Except for a peaty corner for lime-hating plants, the bed contains garden soil mixed with grit. At least that's how it started off eighteen years ago. Invariably at planting time I make up a bucket of fresh compost to suit the plant in question. However, the longer a raised bed has been in existence, the more likely it is to suffer from a buildup of pests and diseases, so little pockets of new soil are always being added. To change all the soil would be impractical, not least because I would be loath to disturb *Tropaeolum polyphyllum*, which occupies the whole of one side and is now so entrenched, shoots even come up in the gravel. The main feature of the opposite side is a group of celmisias (New Zealand daisies). The following are some notable plants in the Sundial Garden.

Tasmanian Christmas bells, *Blandfordia punicea* (a member of the Liliaceae), is described in my dictionary as hardy only to Zone 9 but well suited to pot cultivation. On account of its reputation for being a challenge, I kept it in a pot for some years but it neither grew nor flowered. It cheered up considerably on being planted out—a flowering stem promptly appeared. The flowers, bell-shaped and flared at the rim, are borne in racemes on stiff little stems. Delectable to touch, waxy-textured and polished like satin, they are rosy-scarlet on the outside with yellow underskirts. Evergreen, strap-shaped leaves, under a foot high, are slow to renew themselves. I've never dared to divide it; instinct suggests it would hate to be disturbed. Blandfordia appears to enjoy the same conditions as the celmisias nearby— a peaty mixture kept constantly moist in summer.

OVERLEAF

Tropaeolum poly-phyllum *romping over the raised bed in the Sundial Garden. There are no half measures with this plant—it either proves impossible to establish or becomes a beautiful invader.*

PRECEDING

OVERLEAF

Pulsatilla *'Budapest'*
likes full sun and good
drainage to remind it of
its mountain home.

Sorbus reducta (Zone 6) is the well-known little suckering Himalayan cousin of the mountain ash. The miniature trunks, about two feet tall, bear corymbs of white flowers followed by clusters of relatively large pink berries. The feathery leaves are dark glossy green, turning bronzy-red before falling. The most common clones are the rampaging ones that sucker like ground ivy, but the clone that I have is particularly neat and special, and has never yet produced a sucker. Seeds have been given away several times, but I've yet to hear whether the resulting plants keep to themselves as tidily as their parent.

Salix × *boydii* (Zone 5), a unique and diminutive willow, is extremely slow, only two feet tall after sixteen years. Discovered growing wild in Scotland during the 1880s by William Boyd, it has never been found again; no botanist has yet decided on its precise parentage, although *S. lapponum* × *S. reticulata* has been suggested. Its gnarled branches bear plump, silky "pussies" in spring. Underneath grows a colony of *Primula marginata* 'Linda Pope'. This is a classic among alpine primulas, with tidy rosettes of toothed leaves and lavender-blue flowers with white middles. Less fussy than other cultivars of *P. marginata* (which are quite hardy but better protected from winter wet by being grown under glass; see page 102), this excellent plant should be on the list of the first ten alpines for beginners. Bright red *Primula* × *pubescens* 'Rufus' also gives a good account of itself in the open.

You wouldn't immediately recognize *Polygonatum hookeri* (Zone 6) from the Himalayas and China as a Solomon's seal, for it's barely two inches tall. Pretty lilac-pink flowers, large for the size of the plant, look up at you from tiny clusters of linear leaves. Easy to grow, it forms a slow-spreading mat in a peaty corner.

The pasqueflower called 'Budapest' (perhaps a selection from *Pulsatilla halleri*) is now almost a fable. Via two great plant collectors, Molly Sanderson in Northern Ireland and David Shackleton of Beech Park, I inherited some seedlings of the true plant. The buds, stems, and emerging leaves of these seedlings are covered in gossamer-fine silky hairs. The buds expand before the leaves to gorgeous, pendant, ice-blue flowers, with a central boss of yellow stamens. Some seedlings veer toward lavender and others to almost turquoise, but all are undeniably lovely. *Pulsatilla alpina* subsp. *apiifolia* (Zone 5), the alpine pasqueflower, with pale yellow flowers and ferny leaves grows nearby. All have fluffy, silvery seedheads, and all should never be disturbed. With regard to the white-flowered race of *Pulsatilla vulgaris* (Zone 5), I've ruthlessly had to discard various poor individuals in favor of better ones. Digging up and throwing away plants is always hard; I find it easier to appoint an executioner and then go out for the day.

Unlike the typical blue grape hyacinth, *Muscari macrocarpum* (Zone 7) from the Aegean Islands and Turkey bears racemes of bright yellow, tubby flowers in April, edged with violet-brown at the tips. I used to have this bulb growing at the foot of a sunny wall, but decided it deserved being raised nearer to nose level for the sake of its delicious fra-

grance. The scent, thought to resemble musk, explains the name *Muscari*, from the Persian word *mushk*. Take care not to damage the fleshy roots at the base of the bulb when transplanting.

Codonopsis convolvulacea (Zone 5), a perennial twiner from China and the Himalayas, is represented here by its cultivar 'Alba'. The open, starry, pure white flowers seem too big for the fragile stems. It entwines itself through nearby plants, enjoying the cool root-run beneath their leaves. In danger of being dug up when dormant, the plant has slender stems, agonizingly easy to break by mistake. Be vigilant against slugs nibbling the flowers.

Of those undistinguished nonentities that we lust after, *Scoliopus bigelowii* (Zone 7) of the Liliaceae or Trilliaceae, is the archetypal collector's plant. It is difficult to see. The flowers are camouflaged and close to soil level. It blooms in February, so you have to remember to go and look at it in the middle of winter. And it stinks. Native to moist shady places in California and Oregon, this plant has petals (in fact sepals) finely etched in reddish maroon, and the broad, shining leaves are irregularly blotched with blackish maroon. The stalks bearing the seedheads have a curious habit of arching down toward the soil, as if intent on burying themselves alive.

For some years I grew *Scoliopus bigelowii* in a pot, hoping to give it proper recognition, but even in the alpine house it wasn't exactly showy. Despite these remarks, I consider this a fascinating little plant. Very slow to increase, it grows in the shade of an elderly rhododendron in the lime-free section.

There are numerous other plants in this bed, and countless more have come and gone. I often use it as a temporary recovery area for plants, where I can keep a close eye on their progress.

Tropaeolums

There are no half-measures with *Tropaeolum polyphyllum* (Zone 8). Once it is planted, you either never see it again or it sets off in every direction, draping all nearby plants with elegant trails of glaucous foliage profusely decorated with fat little yellow flowers with conical spurs. (In the wild it is also found in delectable shades of blood orange and mahogany red—let us hope these will soon be introduced into cultivation.) After several attempts, I finally established it here in a sunny, well-drained raised bed.

Gardeners who already have a flourishing colony of this glorious invader from Chile and Argentina are inclined to mutter "Dreadful weed!" as they pull it out by the handful, much to the annoyance of onlookers who would die to own such a plant. In all the years it's been here, I've yet to see a tuber—it seems these work themselves so deeply into the soil, they are impossible to dig up.

Those living in areas colder than Zone 8 should take this behavior as a hint to give *T. polyphyllum* a try—surely tubers so deeply embedded are reasonably safe from frost?

Bedfellows should be chosen with care: Early small bulbs, such as snowdrops and *Iris reticulata*, that go to rest as the tropaeolum emerges, are ideal. The tropaeolum quickly fades after flowering, so the stems may be pulled up to make space for later, sun-loving small herbaceous plants, such as *Origanum laevigatum* (Zone 8).

Tropaeolum speciosum (Zone 8), from Chile, the flame nasturtium or Scottish flame flower, causes instant envy in those who don't have it. It likes a cool, moist place where its slender stems will gently climb or wander in and out of nearby plants, making festoons of brilliant scarlet nasturtium flowers, followed by clusters of vivid blue berries. *Tropaeolum speciosum* may also be slow to establish but, once firmly ensconced, will emerge even in dryish positions nearby. Pull away surplus stems if they are smothering any choice plant.

Tropaeolum tricolorum (Zone 8), from Bolivia and Chile, is a greenhouse treat for spring. The stems, like fine black thread, seem at first as if they cannot decide which way to go, but encouraged by green twine suspended from the roof, can be coaxed to wind clockwise toward the sun. The flowers, like little elfin hats, are a vivacious mix of navy blue, scarlet, and lime, with orange-tipped spurs. The tubers should be kept absolutely dry from the time the stems wither (about May) until they are repotted in September.

The tubers of spring-flowering Tropaeolum tricolorum *should be kept dry in summer and repotted and watered in September.*

The giant Chatham Islands forget-me-not needs a temperate climate, a cool position, and constant protection from slugs.

An Unforgettable Forget-me-not

Myosotidium hortensia (Zone 8), the Chatham Islands forget-me-not, is an extraordinary plant. You might become annoyed by reading further, unless you live in the mildest, dampest, maritime climate (nicely described by Christopher Lloyd, when writing about 45 Sandford Road, as "cough-mixture air"), for it won't thrive anywhere else.

Some people think it is a blue-flowered bergenia. The fleshy, shining, bright green leaves, larger than those of the biggest hosta, are deeply puckered by veins. The corymbs of flowers in late spring are brilliant blue, like waxy large forget-me-nots, dazzling to the eye, but the camera sees it otherwise and refuses to do justice to the color.

Gardening lore has it that myosotidium requires a mulch of seaweed, coming as it does from the shores of the Chatham Islands in the cool South Pacific, where it favors boulder beaches, growing among kelp drift and accumulated seashells. It is an endangered plant, threatened in the wild by the grazing and trampling of introduced pigs and sheep.

One would do anything to please it. I kept it in a pot for years but it never flowered. It needs free-draining, peaty soil, light shade, and diligent protection against slugs, with constant high humidity and a very even temperature. If you can supply all of the above, move on to the next stage: a damp summer and a dry winter. The summer part of the requirements is easily provided in Ireland and the winter part is best organized by making a plastic tent over the plant, allowing plenty of air to enter through the sides.

Although it has the appearance of a plant that you could divide, this is rarely a success. Propagation is best by seed, which is readily produced. A caution here. In summer, you will be itching to cut off any yellowing leaves to keep the plant looking smart. The flower stalks, by now half rotten and lying on the ground, will have clusters of ripening seed, which look very much like blackened seaweed. These stalks are easily detached by mistake from the parent plant, thus losing the year's crop. I've yet to discover whether you're meant to unwrap the seeds from their crinkly, almost woody brown jackets or not; I think the latter is probably correct.

Violas

When you first see a garden, the individual personality of each plant melts away into the overall picture, and you are presented with an extravaganza of flowers, colors, and interwoven leaf patterns, the whole illuminated by the interplay of sun and shadow. But as the immediate impression fades, I like to think that there is an imaginary impresario who is inventing minor surprises to be found around corners—plants to come upon by chance, enjoy for a moment, and then pass by. Thus I have arranged small gatherings of violas around the garden at intervals, their silly faces beaming toward the sun.

The Australian violet, Viola hederacea, in a raised bed on the terrace. An emergency plant is kept in the greenhouse in case the parent succumbs to heavy frost.

To keep proper track of a collection of violas, you have to make yourself think about them in August. Some violas can be easily divided, such as the wonderful, truly perennial horned violet, *Viola cornuta* (Zone 5) and its cultivars. But others are likely to disappear if not regularly renewed from cuttings.

Propagation involves finding that August impossibility—space to insert some outdoor cuttings in a garden already burgeoning with plants. Young stocky cuttings should be taken from the center of the plant (straggly flowering shoots won't root). Sand-lined, finger-deep little trenches are made for them beside the parent plant, and sprinkled often with water.

Cultivars that must be propagated this way include 'Jackanapes', named after Miss Jekyll's pet monkey, with jolly little flowers whose upper two petals are rich, browny red and the bottom three, bright yellow; 'Irish Molly', an extraordinary color, neither bronze nor brown nor green, but all three at once; and 'Molly Sanderson', coal black with a yellow center; plus several other anonymous cultivars.

'Ardross Gem' (violet-blue shading to gold in the center), 'Moonlight' (pale lemon, only flowers once), 'Martin' (deep violet), and others, unlike the fusspots above, are easily divided. 'Maggie Mott' is silvery mauve with a pale cream center. Apparently there are several impostor 'Maggie Motts' around, but the true plant is recognized by its being scented.

Several different fungus diseases attack violas. Control is best effected by moving the plants to a different part of the garden. Space would be easy enough to find if one was looking for it in January, but is nigh impossible in autumn, the best time for establishing good plants for the following year. And it must be premier space at that—the soil cool, moist, and nicely rich.

The Australian violet, *V. hederacea* (Zone 8), is considered tender in Dublin but is so pretty and produces such a seemingly endless succession of flower that it is no trouble to put an emergency plant under glass for the winter. White flowers with charming little purple faces hover on slender stems over low leaf mats. As you would expect from the species epithet, it spreads around like an ivy, rooting as it goes.

I'm always forgetting exactly where I've put spring-flowering *V. sororia* 'Freckles' (Zone 4), an easy, eastern North American plant with a nondescript summer appearance and pale blue flowers delightfully flecked with purplish blue. And *V. biflora* is always missing, presumed lost, until its bright yellow flowers suddenly appear from under a bush. I've almost given up on *V. pedatifida* (Zone 2) for its peculiar, sneaky habit of producing seed without bothering to flower—it has only once produced a flower, in spite of various experiments with potting mixtures.

Viola jooi (Zone 5) is only about three inches high, reliably provides plenty of pink-mauve flowers in spring, seeds itself without becoming a nuisance, and has lived in a sunny raised bed for years. *Viola elatior* (Zone 5), a nice oddity, sometimes called the tree violet, has erect stems to eighteen inches if well fed, and early summer pale blue flowers in the leaf axils.

I have carried on flirtations with many violas over the years. My only excuse for their disappearance is the reputation of some species for being short-lived. And, having seen the rosulate violas of the Andes, which could only have been designed by a Fabergé of the plant world, it is almost a relief that they are reputedly so difficult, it's not even worth trying to grow them.

Deadheading violas is a most soothing occupation. Little physical effort is involved, a sharpened thumbnail is the only tool required, and you can persuade yourself how necessary it is while musing about something else.

Practical Matters

Gardening and pottering are synonymous. It is amazing how long you can spend doing nothing at all. Perhaps the nicest part of gardening is walking round in a daze, wondering at all the beauty that surrounds you. Collectors' gardens are even more hypnotic—you may have decided that the essential task of the day is to check on the health of all your different peonies or whatever, forgetting the multiple diversions you'll meet between one peony and the next.

The problem is chiefly one of application. Often I set off with the firm intention, say, of watering the clematis, only to be so distracted en route that I never get there: Well, there was this rose that needed deadheading, so I had to go back for the secateurs. Going to fetch the secateurs, I notice some seedlings crying out for water. Returning with the watering can, I pass the petunias in even more urgent need of water. I might as well deadhead them while I'm about it. Back in the deadheading mode, off I go again for the secateurs. But on the way to the shed I notice the hairy bittercress, loathsome weed, its seedheads just about to burst. Straight away my mind is on weeds alone; all ideas of deadheading have vanished. Beyond the bittercress is a miniature forest of annual meadow grass—I'd better fetch a bucket. Off again to the shed.

As usual, all buckets have migrated to the compost heap area. Typical. Something at last achieved, I collect a bucket. But on the way to the meadow grass, there is my best delphinium leaning over and just about to snap. Focusing forth-

with on staking alone, a temporary prop is made with the bucket, and I hurry off for stakes and string. At this point the telephone rings. Everything gets forgotten.

Pruning Roses and Clematis

Beginners have too much respect for gardening books, and the old-fashioned head gardener, now extinct, also has a lot to answer for. His position in the hierarchy depended on intimidating both his master and the under-gardeners, and he considered himself the only person fully versed in the mysteries of the ancient art of pruning: It was he, and only he, who dictated when and how this should be done. My theory is that he was so busy with his first loves, the fruit trees and the vegetables, that rose pruning only came up for consideration in March.

I prune the roses in November or December, when I've at last got time to think about them. To prevent winter wind-rock, roses need cutting back in autumn anyway. Furthermore, removing diseased leaves during this operation prevents them from falling to the ground to spread infection for the following year. Autumn pruning also means that I'm not trampling on emerging spring bulbs.

I used to find the subject of rose pruning most alarming. Books were full of little diagrams of the "correct" cut and the "wrong" cut, with much mention of the outward-facing bud. Secateurs in one hand and the book in the other, I would approach the rose, gaze at it in a confused fashion, dither with indecision as to which bud to aim for, and put it off for another day.

Over the years, I have worked out for myself a much simpler rule of thumb: The stronger the shoot, the less I take off; the weaker the shoot, the more I take off. Some of the very old wood is cut to the base. If possible, I cut just above an outward-facing bud, but don't worry too much if there isn't one available. Pruning is all the better for being done on a windy day, when I can see which branches are being chafed. I tie them in then and there. Old-fashioned roses that only flower once, such as 'Charles de Mills' and 'Madame Hardy', get their main annual pruning just after flowering around July. I see no point leaving weak wood for the plant to waste its energy on. The plant itself will benefit from extra light in the center of the bush, while nearby plants will relish the extra space.

In February I go round the roses again, tidying up the earlier pruning. The plants are then fed with bonemeal and mulched with manure or compost. (This is too early to apply chemical fertilizers, which might leach away before the weather warms up. These are applied in April.) In parts of the garden where there are countless spring bulbs, the bonemeal and manure go on before Christmas.

Clematis are another case for discussion. *Clematis viticella* and late-flowering large-flowered cultivars, such as 'Jackmanii', 'Perle d'Azur', and 'Comtesse de Bouchaud', are pruned to within two to three feet of the ground in late autumn. (By tradition, late winter is correct.) The plants are usually covered in fat, green shoots by then, ready to burst into growth. My reasons for pruning at this time are threefold: to stop them from wasting their energy on all those extra buds; to prevent the young shoots from tying themselves into knots in spring; and to get rid of the late-autumn, giant-bird's-nest effect. Be warned, however: Autumn pruning can only be carried out in a temperate climate. I look over the plants again in spring and tidy up the odd forgotten shoot.

My large-flowered clematis, which bloom in early summer, such as 'Lasurstern', 'Nelly Moser', and 'Marie Boisselot', and doubles such as 'Beauty of Worcester' and 'Duchess of Edinburgh', are pruned very lightly: I cut them back to the first healthy bud and take out dead wood. Dealing with these is a slow job and I can do it properly only when not preoccupied with something else. I try to train the stems at the same time, so that they're nicely spread out. Spring-flowering *Clematis alpina, C. montana,* and *C. macropetala* are never pruned.

Weeding

The lazier you are, the more diligently you should weed, for each weed taken out before it sets seed allows a few more minutes' lazing time. Some gardeners enjoy a wheelbarrow full of hefty weeds, and heaps of the enemy lying wilting in the sun, but I like to collect them when they're so small that there's no more than a bucketful per large bed. By weeding little and often instead of having an occasional blitz, I'm in close contact with the plants, and can notice a plant that needs watering, propagating, or rescuing to intensive care in a pot. A great plantsman once told me that weeding was the best possible gardening—it keeps you in touch with your plants.

Incidentally, I've always been amused by people who remark, "What excellent maintenance you have!" It implies that there is nothing of artistic merit in the garden, either in the selection of plants or in their arrangement. Furthermore, this comment suggests that the only reason the garden is tidy and weed-free is because you have spent masses of money with a maintenance contractor. I like it.

Deadheading

This can be thought of in two different ways—"emergency" and "serious." The former can be attended to while conducting a conversation, as you idly pluck off faded roses or snatch the tops of dahlias. The latter is more systematic, and takes place once a week in summer, when the roses are snipped correctly (just above the second or third leaf below the deadhead), old stems of herbaceous plants are cut to ground level if necessary, and the old flower stems of dahlias are cut off to the top of the foliage, instead of leaving lots of unsightly stalks. Late summer deadheading involves more than just taking off faded flowers—time spent tweaking off yellowing leaves quickly freshens up the garden's end-of-season appearance.

The Annual Evaluation of the Garden

I love my plants. I want to grow healthy plants, and the joy of owning a rare specimen is nothing if it's only a poor little stick of a thing with three limp leaves and an outsize label. I want to display plants well, too, so that their best attributes of flower, leaf, and habit are shown to advantage. I also want to position them so as to add to the overall picture.

My most important gardening operation takes place in autumn. Notebook in hand, standing beside every single plant in the garden, from alpines and herbaceous perennials to shrubs and trees, I conduct a rigorous inquisition. I force myself to take a good, hard look at the plant (I think many gardeners look at their plants, but don't actually see them.) I then ask myself the following questions.

"Do I like this plant?" The obvious answer, "Yes, of course I do, or it wouldn't be here," isn't necessarily true. The plant may have been glowingly described in a catalog but doesn't live up to its reputation. Or my taste may have changed. Or, yes, it *is* a lovely plant, but it is obviously unhappy here and must be given away to a larger or milder garden, or one with acid soil. Or the plant is nice but a geriatric, better replaced by a youngster. Euthanasia is always acceptable in the well-run garden. Many plants are full of memories of the gardening friends who gave them, but good gardeners could only approve of this cycle of renewal; their names live on in the form of the young plant.

Still staring at the plant, I continue: "Does it need propagating?" This may be necessary either because I like it so much that I want more of it, or because I don't like it but someone else might. (It would stop me feeling guilty if I gave away a rooted cutting.) The plant may not be flourishing and might be invigorated by a move. Herbaceous plants in particular rapidly respond to division and a move to fresh soil.

Should I decide to dig up some plant, there is nothing more annoying than somebody muttering, "What a shame," "Poor thing," "So pretty in the spring," and so on. What I want at this stage is the Queen of Hearts "stamping about, and shouting, 'Off with his head!'…about once in a minute." This would be much more helpful.

The inquisition continues with this litany:

"Is the plant in the right place? Is it getting enough sun, shade, light, moisture? Is it squashing its neighbors? Is it suffering from too much competition? Does it enhance or detract from plants nearby?"

With an ever-increasing number of plants to move, I begin transplanting in August and aim to finish by the end of October. Tender plants wait until spring, but it is then that my worst mistakes are made. I misjudge a plant's eventual size, and what appears to be an empty space proves to be quite the reverse. Spring bulbs are moved just after flowering, when obvious gaps, invisible in summer, present themselves.

Some plants spend autumn in the wheelbarrow, being trundled up and down, as I try to decide on the right place to put them. Sometimes, in a flash of inspiration, a decision is made right away, but more often than not, back they go in the barrow to remain in limbo for weeks.

My fundamental rule of gardening is, "When in doubt about a plant, move it." I'm trying to provide each and every plant with the best possible cultural conditions. At the same time, I'm trying to create a scene that is beautiful when viewed as a whole. My only hope of achieving this marvelously pretentious ideal is to constantly reshuffle the plants—forever reorganizing their heights, colors, and leaf shapes—in a never-ending (but highly enjoyable) attempt at the impossible.

OVERLEAF

The terrace under snow.

Bibliography

Armitage, Allan M. *Herbaceous Perennial Plants.* Athens: Varsity Press, Inc., 1989.

Beales, Peter. *Classic Roses.* New York: Holt, Rinehart and Winston, 1985.

Brickell, Christopher, and Fay Sharman. *The Vanishing Garden.* London: John Murray, 1986.

Clausen, Ruth Rogers, and Nicholas H. Ekstrom. *Perennials for American Gardens.* New York: Random House, 1989.

Colvin, Christina and Charles Nelson. "Building Castles of Flowers: Maria Edgeworth as Gardener." *Garden History, The Journal of the Garden History Society* 16 (Spring 1988).

Dickerson, Brent. *The Old Rose Advisor.* Portland, OR: Timber Press, 1992.

Huxley, Anthony, ed. *The New Royal Horticultural Society Dictionary of Gardening.* London and Basingstoke: Macmillan Press Ltd., 1992.

Jekyll, Gertrude. *Colour Schemes for the Flower Garden.* London: Country Life, 1925.

Lloyd, Christopher. *Clematis.* London: Collins, 1977.

Lord, Tony, ed. and Chris Philip, comp. *The Plant Finder 1994/95.* London: Moorland Publishing Co. Ltd.

Nelson, E. Charles. *An Irish Flower Garden.* Kilkenny: Boethius Press, 1984.

Pankhurst, Alex. *Who Does Your Garden Grow?* Colchester: Earl's Eye Publishing, 1992.

Phillips, Roger, and Martyn Rix. *Perennials.* Vol. 1, *Early Perennials,* and Vol. 2, *Late Perennials.* London: Pan Books, 1991.

Thomas, Graham Stuart. *Perennial Garden Plants or The Modern Florilegium.* London: J. M. Dent, 1990.

Index

Zone Map

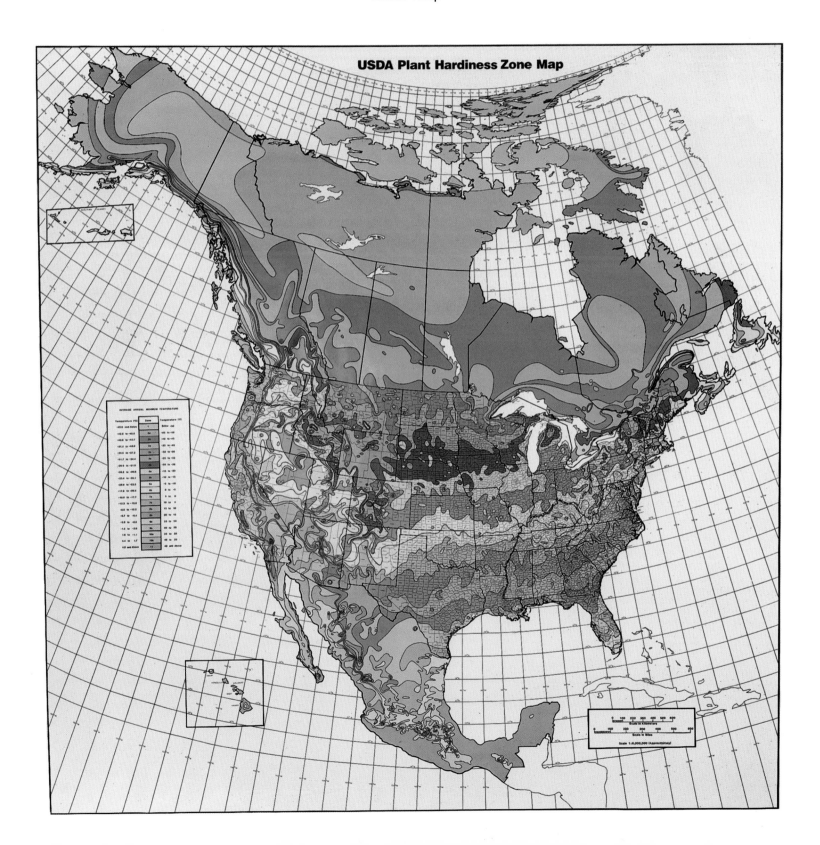

With special thanks to Val, my husband, and a big thank you to

Diane Tomlinson, Mary Rowe, Tom Fisher, Charles Nelson,

Jennie McGregor Bernard, and John Meils.

Anthemis punctata *subsp.* cupaniana *should be cut back hard after flowering; it will then rapidly renew itself.*

Designed by Gates Sisters Studio